CECIL MURPHEY

NEW YORK TIMES BESTSELLING WRITER, *90 Minutes in Heaven*

KNOWING
GOD
KNOWING
MYSELF

An Invitation to Daily Discovery

Gospel Light

From Gospel Light
Ventura, California, U.S.A.

Published by Regal
From Gospel Light
Ventura, California, U.S.A.
www.regalbooks.com
Printed in the U.S.A.

Library of Congress Cataloging-in-Publication Data
Murphey, Cecil.
Knowing God, knowing myself : an invitation to daily discovery / Cecil Murphey.
p. cm.
ISBN 978-0-8307-5673-5 (trade paper)
1. Spiritual life—Christianity. I. Title.
BV4501.3.M865 2010
248.4—dc22
2010035101

1 2 3 4 5 6 7 8 9 10 11 12 13 14 / 20 19 18 17 16 15 14 13 12 11 10

A few names have been changed in this book to protect the privacy of the individuals.

Rights for publishing this book outside the U.S.A. or in non-English languages are
administered by Gospel Light Worldwide, an international not-for-profit ministry.
For additional information, please visit www.glww.org, email info@glww.org, or write
to Gospel Light Worldwide, 1957 Eastman Avenue, Ventura, CA 93003, U.S.A.

To order copies of this book and other Regal products in bulk quantities,
please contact us at 1-800-446-7735.

Contents

ACKNOWLEDGMENTS

Knowing God isn't a solitary experience. Others guide us in our spiritual growth. I owe much to many who have held my hand, challenged me, rebuked me, and especially those who loved me.

I could go all the way back to my childhood and my Sunday School teacher Marie Garbie, who loved me and prayed for me long before I opened myself to God.

Although it's impossible to list them, I'm grateful to every one who nudged me closer to God. But most important, I have to thank Shirley, my wife. She taught me about God's love and forgiveness before I married her. By her lifestyle she continues to help me know myself and to know God.

Knowing God

(An Introduction)

For most of my adult life, I've yearned to experience an intimacy with God. That search began in my early twenties when, as an agnostic, I underwent a profound spiritual awakening. In the process of discovering God, I also learned about myself. I went from calling myself an agnostic to becoming a serious Christian. Several years later, I realized that knowing God and knowing myself went together. We need both self-knowledge and divine knowledge to progress.

As I've continued to follow my spiritual journey, I realize that for those of us who seek to know ourselves and to know God, the path may be different but we have much in common. St. Teresa of Avila said it better than I can: "We shall never succeed in knowing ourselves unless we seek to know God."

Most of my writing comes out of discoveries in my search for a more meaningful, authentic spiritual life. As I continue to mature, I'm aware how much I want to share with others who yearn for deeper self-knowledge and more of God.

I've hit many spiritual low points; my life hasn't been one glorious, triumphant upward trek. In fact, I've learned most of my lessons through pain, failure and weakness. Although this constant yearning to understand the Lord has permeated my life, I take no credit for that: I believe that God has filled my heart with that desire. He has never given up on me nor allowed me to give up.

My conversion began after I read Paul's quotation from Isaiah: "I have been found by those who did not seek me; I have shown myself to those who did not ask for me" (Rom. 10:20, *RSV*).

I graduated from college with a major in religion, earned a master's degree in education from a large university and went on to seminary for a second master's degree. Although I'm grateful for the education, none of my academic background satisfied my spiritual yearnings. My instructors provided information, handed me research tools and encouraged me to think and read more. My soul continued to yearn for an increasing intimacy with the Divine One.

I served as a missionary in Kenya for six years. Those years transformed my training into practical living. During our time in Africa, I spent most evenings reading theology. Many other nights I wrestled with a burning desire to know God more. "Teach me, lead me, guide me," was my frequent cry. Or I quoted Paul's words, "That I may know him" (Phil. 3:10, *RSV*).

For 14 years, I pastored congregations in the metro-Atlanta area. As I reached out to hurting people, I faced many of my own issues. While I struggled with my own problems as well as helping others, I slowly grew in my understanding of God.

I continue to read widely. Although I found much help from others who had blazed the spiritual trails before me, I realized I had to determine my own path and find my own process. Not everyone may consider my methods orthodox, but they work for me, and I've discovered a number of ways that have fostered my spiritual growth.

One major way I express my faith is by writing aphorisms—succinct statements that express things I've learned or want to learn.

I pray or meditate daily on my briefly stated petitions. I write them on three-by-five-inch index cards and pray such prayers. This method works for me, and I want to share it with others.

Each chapter of this book contains a prayer or an affirmation. For me, affirmation is a form of prayer. When I repeat such statements, I am petitioning God to make them a reality in my life. Each day I continue to pray them (and sometimes modify them) until I know they have become part of me or until God has granted me my petitions.

I'll never arrive at a place where I know everything, but that's still my goal anyway. I start to get close, and then unexplored spiritual areas cry out to me—and in some instances I've been shocked at my discoveries. As soon as I grasp a sacred truth and apply what I've learned, something new and unexplored occurs to me.

The constant challenges make my spiritual quest exciting, and it assures me that I may be closer to the original apostles, the ancient church fathers and Middle-Ages mystics than I thought. My language differs greatly and the issues I face seem outwardly different. But as I read their words and translate them into the modern world, I feel as if I have linked hands with them.

The Process and the Results

I used to be afraid to anticipate the abundance of joy and happiness that lay ahead if my plans came to fruition. *What if it doesn't happen?* I'd ask, and that question would make me hold back. *What if I work on this project, give myself to it totally, and it fails?*

"What if I get a degree and no one hires me?" a student asked.

"What if I start an on-line store and I lose everything?" an entrepreneur asked.

"What if I fall in love and the relationship falls apart?" the eager young woman asked.

"It's better to be sure it will succeed before I undertake anything," I said.

I was wrong.

Success isn't as important as we make it out to be. I've met a number of successful-but-miserable people.

For more than 20 years, I've been a co-writer and ghostwriter for celebrities. Having money or fame didn't make any of them happy. They may enjoy life but it wasn't because of outward advantages. Happiness and joy grow from within. But I didn't always know that.

For years I heard clever sayings about how the journey was the reward and not the destination. I smiled as I read those wise sayings. But I didn't believe them. Instead, I thought, *If the end—a successful finish—isn't significant, why set goals or attempt to move ahead?*

A few years ago I began to change the way I thought about success and failure. I stopped asking myself, *What happens if I fail?* Even if I don't get the results I want, I can still have fun in the process.

I want to enjoy my life, I told myself, *regardless of results. Maybe the journey is the joyful place.*

Sometimes I'm a little slow to figure things out, but here's the conclusion I finally accepted for myself and offer to anyone else who wants to enjoy life: Find the things about which you are passionate. We can give ourselves to enjoying those tasks, jobs or professions. If we don't find pleasure in what we're doing, maybe we need to think about doing something else. I found my greatest joy in writing; others have experienced joy in other areas.

During my early pastoral days, a carpenter named Les joined our congregation. One time he said something like this, "When I look at my hands, I feel God made them big so I can build things." A bank teller said, "When I get to the end of the day and all my figures balance, I relax. I know I've done a good job."

No matter what our passion, it's individual and it's what we feel internally—an inner peace. The answer isn't what others say, such as, "Oh, you'd be so good at . . ."

When I was in seminary, a highly successful entrepreneur offered me a job to manage a chain of hotels in Argentina. "You have the right personality for that kind of job." And he hinted at a big salary. But I felt no passion toward the task and I turned it down.

If we want to enjoy life, it's not in accumulating trophies of big houses, expensive cars or profitable investments. The joy comes in following our inner desires. If we give our best to whatever it is, we can enjoy the process.

I want to give you permission to dream—just as I gave myself the freedom to do that. Think passionate and powerful thoughts about your life. Enjoy the excitement that comes when you throw your energies into a project. Why not do your best regardless of how things turn out?

We can't determine the outcome no matter how hard we try. In the church, haven't we always said that ultimately everything is in God's hands? However, I've noticed that we usually remind others of that after they've failed. Why not focus on the thrill of unleashing our energies right now?

For example, my friend and editor Nick Harrison asked me if I had a book within me, a passion that I had never had fulfilled.

"Yes," I told him, "I have one." And I told him about it.

At least a decade ago, I wrote a historical novel set in the 1920s. Publisher after publisher turned it down. Some liked the book but they didn't do historical fiction (anything in the early twentieth century they now considered historical). It was set in Oklahoma during the dust bowl and Great Depression, and they didn't do books about the Southwest. A few didn't like my writing; others simply said, "It's not for us."

So far no publisher has accepted the book, and it may never go into print. I wish it would, because I am a writer and I write books to sell to publishing houses. I've written it with 200,000 words; revised it; made it into a trilogy. I've changed a few characters and added others, but the basic story is the same.

"What a waste of effort," one of my writer friends said.

"Certainly not! This is my passion!" I said before I thought about my response. "I've loved the process. I keep learning about the craft, and in the process of writing, God becomes more real to me and I learn more about myself."

Those words shocked me: I hadn't said them to anyone or been conscious of them, but I knew I spoke the truth to my friend.

I also decided that I want to live with that passion—giving everything I have to all projects, every venture and each idea.

Instead of looking to the future—anticipating the failure or success of the activity—what if we looked at activities as a place on which to heap our passion? *The doing is our responsibility; the result is God's responsibility.*

Think about yourself. Because you've been disappointed, you may be afraid to hope or feel enthusiasm over possibilities. *I've been shot down before,* you tell yourself. Yes, disappointment may strike repeatedly, but why not enjoy giving yourself to something you love doing? Why not anticipate having fun on the journey? Why not consider the immense, enriching experience right now?

Suppose your efforts fail. What have you lost? Time perhaps. But can it be wasted if you had fun along the way?

Why not throw yourself into the venture and dream of all the wonderful things that lie ahead? If they don't happen, it's all right, and you enjoyed that phase of the journey. You've done your best. Now you can prepare for and enjoy the next task.

What is one dream (or one project, task or opportunity) that could bring you great joy and satisfaction? What is one unfulfilled dream you have—a dream that is yet possible to fulfill? Tell God and yourself how passionately you feel about that dream.

> *God, enable me to fulfill this dream.*
> *If I'm not to find fulfillment in this dream, encourage me*
> *to know that I'm doing what excites me, and in the*
> *process I'm drawing closer to you.*

I've found peace and greater joy by repeating these words:

> *I am passionately involved in the process;*
> *I am emotionally detached from the result.*

2

Our Unhealed Parts

During my days in the Navy, I had one of those slow, quiet conversions. God changed my life, and later I found a church where I felt I belonged. I also joined in a number of Christian fellowships. For several months a small group of us met almost every morning in the balcony of the base chapel. Barry Grahl taught me to memorize Bible verses; Chaplain Paul Reiss pushed me to study the Bible. My best friend, John Burbank, listened to my endless questions as I sought to grow.

Like most zealous converts, I talked to others about my newfound faith. Several of those who had served with me before my conversion openly spoke of the difference in my life.

"I'm totally given to God," I said to John. And to my way of thinking, I meant that. John tried to caution me because he knew more theology than I did and understood more about sinful humanity.

I boasted that day—although I didn't see it as anything except telling what I believed was true. In those early days, life was wonderful and I lived with the zeal of a new convert. We used to sing a chorus called, "It's Bubbling." I would say that I was bubbling, and Barry insisted he was tingling.

I worked in an office where we did court martial reviews. One morning I came in after having been gone on a week's leave, and a sailor named Ike told me what he had done while I had been gone. He hadn't known the proper procedure and should have left it for me. Instead, he took over and made a terrible mess.

I explained in lengthy detail what he had done wrong. Ike stared at me and said nothing. Just then, I turned around. A sailor named Darrel, whom I had invited to join our morning prayer group, stood at the door.

He said, "I didn't think I'd ever hear you talk that way! If that's what being a Christian is, I'm not interested." Then he turned and hurried away.

I stood there, trying to figure out what he meant. I had talked honestly to Ike. I thought over what I had said and couldn't see what was so upsetting.

What was wrong? I honestly didn't know. I didn't figure it out that day or for many, many days later. A decade later, my wife gently chided me for being angry and harsh with a group of giggling girls in church.

"Angry? I wasn't angry—"

"You were," she said quietly as we got into the car. She didn't intend to argue with me but only to point out something.

I would have asked, "Are you sure?" but my wife wouldn't have said those words without being certain. For the next 10 minutes of driving home, and for two hours later that afternoon, I mentally rehearsed that scene as I walked through our neighborhood. "How could she have thought I was angry and harsh?" I asked aloud.

It took almost the entire two hours of walking before I realized something: *I had been angry.* I had raised my voice (or did I yell?) and my face must have shown how I really felt.

I hadn't been aware.

I remember the incident so vividly because Shirley taught me an invaluable lesson even though that wasn't what she intended. Until that Sunday when she chided me, I could have stood before God, Shirley, the giggling girls and our pastor and said, "I'm not angry about anything."

But I had been angry. Worse, I had been angry and didn't know it.

That was the first time I became aware of spiritual blind spots, and I continue to find them. I had to learn to listen to my words and become aware of the expressions on my face. Later, when I asked, Shirley spoke about my scowl.

I haven't mastered my anger, but I've learned something significant: I don't know parts of myself—my blind spots—or as Psalm 19:12 calls it, my "hidden faults." Those are my failures and sins of which I'm not aware.

Shirley opened a door to my unknown self—the things hidden to me. It's taken me years but I finally realized something and I said it aloud to David Morgan, my long-time accountability partner-friend. "I'm an angry person; I come from an angry family; and I'm afraid to admit my anger to myself."

That confession was the beginning of healing for me. I also began to understand the origin of my anger. My father was a quiet, self-controlled man until about his third beer. That's when he became angry and physically abusive, even when I had no idea of the reason for the beating he gave me. I didn't understand that the beer released his inhibitions and allowed his rage to erupt. Somehow I accepted the inner message that I couldn't express anger. If I did, I'd erupt like Dad.

I had to receive healing—and it's still ongoing in my life. Therefore, here's a simple prayer I use almost every day: "Heal the parts of me that don't want to be healed."

All of us have parts that aren't healed—the things we deny about ourselves. We haven't come to terms with our deepest, inmost parts. Some call it the unconscious self—the powerful forces within us that act without our awareness. Regardless of what we name it, most of us seem afraid that they'll overwhelm us, hurt too much if we face the truth or spoil our self-image of being deeply spiritual.

Because we're children of the always-loving God, we need to remind ourselves that this same God will prepare us to "hear" the truth and lead us to accept those unhealed parts. Even more wonderful, the Lover of our Souls holds our hands as we walk toward deliverance.

Some people don't want to know the truth about themselves—especially their hidden weaknesses. And it's not my responsibility to force them. God loves all of us and wants our spiritual healing even if we pull back.

I sometimes tell people to pray, "God, heal the parts of me that don't want to be healed." Then I urge them to listen—no matter how many times they have to go through this process.

We need to learn to trust that whatever understanding we receive about our unhealed parts can also give us confidence: It means the Lord is ready to heal.

I still ask myself regularly: "What parts of you need healing?"

God, heal the parts of me that don't want to be healed.

3

Being Admired

Who doesn't enjoy receiving compliments? We may blush or try to deflect the words, but inwardly we're pleased. We're delighted that someone is aware of what we've said or done.

That's being human, and we need affirmation from others. To receive those compliments too often or too profusely can ruin us. They used to talk about big-headed celebrities because they started to believe their press releases—the very things created to make them look good.

If we hear those compliments often enough, we can begin to feel smug or superior to others, and that results in our becoming arrogant or difficult to get along with. Most of us know people like that. As a writer, I've worked with a few celebrities for whom I feel sorry. They have surrounded themselves with sycophants who say the right words and consistently tell them how wonderful they are.

The celebrities live beyond the world of most of us, but many of us need to face a more subtle form of the same problem. We have developed an image—the way people see us at church, at work or in the neighborhood. If it's a good image, we work hard to protect (and enhance) it.

Although that image may be accurate, it's not the real us—at best, it reflects part of who we are. I'll explain it this way. Perhaps a decade ago, people began to call me kind, and one woman insisted I was a compassionate person. People may have spoken that way earlier, but I began to *hear* them.

"Am I really like that?" I asked Shirley.

"Yes, you are," my wife said and touched my cheek. "But that's not all you are."

I laughed and have repeated those words to myself many times. Shirley said it exactly right for me. What those people saw and admired was good, and it *is* part of who I am. I'm slightly uncomfortable with some of the words, but I accept them.

The trouble begins with hearing those compliments too often. The more we hear such statements, the more we tend to accept and believe them.

I'll explain it by telling you about Steve, who is bright, informed and a reader of dozens of newspapers and online news sites each day. He's up on all the current books that relate to business, medicine, sports or world affairs. Steve isn't smug about it, but he's the man who knows details and can explain almost anything. He's the resource person and the trivia expert.

That's also Steve's image. He has to stay at his reading and research because he has an image to protect. He falls into the pit of depression when others know information he doesn't.

Melva is an incredibly efficient woman and she doesn't make mistakes. On those rare occasions when someone challenges her and she is wrong, Melva can rationalize so it doesn't reflect on her. In a moment of weakness, she once said, "I hate for anyone to think of me as inefficient." To her, one mistake equals inefficiency.

Those are only two examples, but my assumption is that all of us have such images about ourselves. Whatever the image is, it helps to define us but can also enslave us. We're forced to live up to that partially true picture of ourselves.

Years ago, when I began to ghostwrite, I wrote the autobiography of a famous country-and-western singer. At one point in his career, he became side-tracked with drugs and it took him years to kick the habit.

When I spoke to the singer's wife about her perspective on the drugs, she made a comment that says it well. "Performers can't have a bad day. People pay to hear them, and the singers can't say, 'I'm tired.' They have to perform. And many of them use drugs so they can live up to the expectation of others."

Most of us don't rely on drugs to keep us performing and protecting our image; however, we work hard to safeguard that concept of whom people perceive us to be.

A businessman told me that for years he didn't speak up in company discussions. Early in his career, his boss branded him as a special employee because he was the man who "wears well, takes everything in stride and never gets ruffled." When we spoke about guarding his image, his eyes lit up and he said, "I know what I have to do to change that perception."

I didn't see him again for at least a year. At that time, we talked about his iconic status and he laughed. "That wasn't who I really was. I was afraid—I didn't want others to think less of me and I couldn't allow myself to lose face. I wanted them to accept me and appreciate me as the steady person on the team." He smiled, winked and said, "I've learned to raise my voice and make objections when I need to do that."

He said, "My boss hasn't complimented me on my change, but I like myself better."

He illustrates the point for me. We can get so caught up in trying to be the spiritual being, the true Christian leader, the compassionate Christian who always has time for everyone that we get close to worshiping a false god. We lose divine blessings because we've lost touch with our true identity. Even if what others said is true, it's only part of the truth and not the total person. Or as Shirley put it, "That's not all you are."

For the past five years I've worked to become transparent. I want people to accept me as I truly am or—this is the painful part—that means they may reject me for who I am. I don't want to be the person who says to himself, *They're applauding me for what I do, but if they knew who I really am, would they still applaud?*

Remember when Internet geeks spoke about WYSIWYG? That means "What you see is what you get." I like that, and I'd like WYSIWYG to become my slogan.

*Loving God, it's so easy to get caught up in being
perceived as a spiritual person or conforming to an image;
help me to be as true to myself and to you as I can.*

*I'd rather be disliked for who I am than to be
admired for who I'm not.*

About that Anger

Dick had raged long enough (although he wouldn't have used that term) until I said, "You're really upset, aren't you?"

"And I have good reason to be angry," he replied. Dick had yelled about unemployment, the corrupt politicians and a lengthy rant that also provided endless details about the way the pastor and members of his church had failed him. He went on a second verbal blast.

When his monologue finally ran down, I said to him, "I've learned something important about my anger. I'm willing to share it with you if you'd like."

Dick shrugged.

"I can give it to you in one sentence."

"Try me."

"I'm seldom angry about what I think I'm angry about."

He stared blankly and I repeated my aphorism. "I don't get it. I *know* what I'm angry about."

"Do you?" I asked. I've known Dick for enough years that I can challenge him and he won't swing that powerful fist toward my face.

He started complaining again—although I'd heard it the first time.

I held up my hand and said, "I wonder if that's what really upsets you." I let those words hang before I said, "You've mentioned three major things that make you angry before you mentioned the church. Maybe that's correct or maybe . . ."

"Maybe what?"

"Maybe they're easy targets. Maybe they're safe to get angry about." I didn't wait for Dick to refute my statements. "I used to get angry a lot until I admitted that the object of my anger wasn't always the true object."

"So you think I pick easy, defenseless targets?"

"Not intentionally," I said.

Again, Dick shrugged.

Dick and I sat quietly. His large clock ticked several minutes.

"So you think that instead of facing what really upsets me, I reroute it and blow up where it's safe—"

"Or where you can get away with it."

"Sounds pretty good," he said. "How did you figure that out?"

"Experience. Sad, sad experience." I told Dick a biblical story—that was the easy way to win him over. I told him about Jonah—and, of course, he knew the whale story. "But that's not the real story," I said.

The real message of the book of Jonah is that God called the man to go to the city of Nineveh, capitol of the Assyrian empire and a rising world power. The book of Jonah doesn't record much about the wickedness, but the prophet Nahum provides details.

Jonah refused to obey the Lord and ran away. That's the whale story and that covers only chapters 1 and 2. Chapters 3 and 4 are the real message.

Jonah finally obeyed. He walked into the city and "he shouted to the crowds: 'Forty days from now Nineveh will be destroyed'" (Jon. 3:4).

The king heard the pronouncement and commanded the people to repent—and they did. Consequently, God spared the city.

Chapter 4 gives us a true picture of Jonah. "This change of plans greatly upset Jonah, and he became very angry" (4:1). He admitted that God was compassionate and would spare the people. In anger the prophet went to the west side of the city and waited.

That night God "arranged for a leafy plant to grow there, and soon it spread its broad leaves over Jonah's head, shading him from the sun. This eased his discomfort, and Jonah was very grateful. But God also arranged for a worm! The next morning at dawn the worm ate the stem of the plant so that it withered away. And as the sun grew hot, God arranged for a scorching east wind to blow on Jonah. The sun beat down on his head until he grew faint and wished to die. 'Death is certainly better than living like this!' he exclaimed" (4:6-8).

God asks the prophet, "Is it right for you to be angry because the plant died?" (v. 9). And Jonah insists he has that right.

God challenged Jonah. "You feel sorry about the plant, though you did nothing to put it there. It came quickly and died quickly. But Nineveh has more than 120,000 people living in spiritual darkness, not to mention all the animals. Shouldn't I feel sorry for such a great city?" (vv. 10-11).

Jonah was angry because the plant died, but that wasn't the real cause of his anger. His fight was with God. My assumption is that Jonah wasn't able to say, "You made a fool out of me and made me lose face. You told me to pronounce destruction and now you go ahead and save them."

After I finished the story, I smiled at Dick.

"Maybe that's right," he said.

"I don't have to be right," I said, "but I hope that when you're angry, you'll ask yourself a question: Am I angry about the plant dying or about God showing mercy?" (Dick especially appreciates it when I talk to him using biblical images.)

I suppose most of us are like Dick and even like Jonah. It's easier to get angry at people and objects that can't retaliate than it is to admit the true cause of our anger. It's also easier to blame circumstances and other people than it is to accept blame for our failures.

I am seldom angry about what I think I am angry about.

5

Reexamining the Past

While our grandson Brett was living with us, one Sunday morning he moved slowly and we had to hurry to get to Sunday School on time. He got into the backseat, remembered something and ran back to get it. He left the car door open.

Because we were late, I decided to back out and wait in the driveway until Brett came back. I backed out, but the open car door hit the side of the garage and I heard a terrible crunch. The car door was bent and it ruined the panel for our garage door. I was able to drive, but I could barely keep Brett's door closed.

I felt terrible for doing such a dumb thing and I was annoyed with myself. It wasn't Brett's fault and I didn't blame him. As I drove to church, I kept thinking about the minor accident. If only I had paid more attention . . . if only I had remembered the open door . . . if only I had waited about 10 seconds . . .

"Inside your head you keep going over what happened, don't you?" Brett asked.

I nodded, but I also thought about the words of that teenage boy. He was right. Although it had been a minor accident, my mind didn't want to let go. My thoughts flashed on other times when I had done something stupid, been wrong or hurt another person's feelings. On those occasions, I had also replayed the scenes inside my head.

As I reviewed the accident, I thought of what had happened on those other occasions. As in the past, I repeatedly focused my thoughts on how I might have done things differently.

The morning of the car accident, however, I realized something. No matter how many times I reviewed the crunching of my car door, no matter how many things I realized that I could have done differently, nothing was going to change.

In that instant, an aphorism came to me: *No matter how many times I examine the past, there's nothing I can do to make it different.*

As those words filled my mind, they seemed obvious. Maybe, but I hadn't listened before. And I'm not alone. I've met a number of people who live in the past—usually because of past mistakes or decisions—and they can't forgive themselves.

When I was a student pastor, a Vietnam vet started attending our church. Johnny was an alcoholic who hadn't fully recovered. One time he told me his story: "My best buddy was right in front of me as we marched along. He stepped on a bomb and was killed instantly." Tears filled his eyes and he said, "I don't know how it happened, but I was supposed to have been the point man. I was the one who should have died."

I don't know what happened to Johnny, but in the two years I was there, he never got beyond his guilt. His story is extreme, but all of us are a bit like Johnny. We tend to focus on what might have been and how we might have reacted differently if we could do it again. But no matter how intensely we go over the past or how often we rehearse it, the past is still the past and it won't change.

> *No matter how many times I examine the past,*
> *there's nothing I can do to make it different.*

6

Too Much to Do

Like many people, my days are full. I have too many things I want to accomplish. I'm also a list maker and I write the tasks on a yellow lined tablet and keep it on my desk where I'll see it several times during the day. As I complete each item, I draw a thick, black line through the words and smile at my accomplishment.

That's the good part, but some days I've felt overwhelmed. As the saying goes, "So much to do, so little time to do it." *How can I possibly get everything done today?* I ask myself. I know many other people struggle over the same problem.

Our culture pushes us to rush, to hurry, to multitask so we can accomplish more. Because of technology, we can do more things than previous generations, but we tend to feel we've accomplished less because we leave too many things undone.

At the end of each day, I turned off my computer and inwardly moaned because I still had many tasks I hadn't completed. I didn't want more hours in my day, as I've heard some people say wistfully; I simply wanted more control over what I had to do. I liked my work and I didn't want to have less; I wanted to complete everything on my list and make it the best I could do.

Here's how I found help: I'm a runner, and I got into the habit of being on the pavement around 5:00 each morning so I could work all day and not be interrupted by having to exercise. (I also knew that if I waited until the middle of the day I'd decide my work was more urgent and I wouldn't exercise.) It was a good idea—and it's still my daily habit—but it didn't enable me to finish everything that day. The list grew longer and the frustration more frequent.

One morning during my run, I grumbled to God about all the things I had to finish that day. I planned to run my normal six miles but I couldn't forget the lengthy number of items on the yellow pad. They seemed to have grown exponentially over the past few days. *I'll cut the run down to three miles,* I thought, because of all the things waiting for me.

Seconds before I decided to turn around, however, a thought flashed through my mind: *Today I have time to do everything I need to do today.*

The repetition of the word "today" struck me as the important aspect of the sentence. The words sounded incredibly simple (and they are), and they were precisely what I needed to tell myself. I had set up self-imposed deadlines on projects and urgent tasks that I didn't want to put off for another day. The push to get things done came from some internal demand and certainly not from God. For example, I hated to leave unanswered email on my computer more than a few hours and felt I *had* to respond to it immediately.

As I ran, I repeated the words aloud: "Today I have time to do everything I need to do today." I yelled thanks to God as I continued my six-mile run.

From then on, that insight became part of my daily prayers: *God, help me remember that today I have time to do everything I need to do today.*

I still struggle with the same issue, but repeating those words reminds me that I need to focus only on today and not worry about what I can't get done.

My simple prayer sounds a little like something Jesus said: "So don't worry about tomorrow, for tomorrow will bring its own worries. Today's trouble is enough for today" (Matt. 6:34).

Yes, God, today I can handle what I need to do today.

Today I have time to do everything I need to do today.

7

Rethinking Our Focus

Our house burned to the ground in 2007, and we lost everything we'd accumulated through the years. We'd been comfortable in our house and I enjoyed my fairly large library.

Now everything was gone, and it meant starting over. Not only in rebuilding, but the situation forced us to think about every item of furniture. Previously, we'd bought a few items at a time and now we had to think of furnishing an entire house.

More than books or tables, we were starting over again with new computers, dishes and clothes. Shirley couldn't reach for oregano or dill because we didn't have any. I didn't have a stapler or paper clips.

That's when I realized something significant: I could focus on those things taken from us or I could realize that loss also brings freedom. I could start over in many ways.

I want to be clear that Shirley and I felt a sense of loss and we had sad moments when we realized that some items were not replaceable, such as photographs, a favorite shirt or music CDs. I allowed myself time to think about those things and regret what we had lost, but I didn't want the losses of the past to take up permanent residence.

Besides the things involved with the house, I decided that I was starting new in almost every area of my life and I could make changes. One thing I wanted to rethink was my relationships. I could leave behind the individuals who had once been friends but the friendship demanded high maintenance. I didn't have to focus on taking care of them or staying around professional colleagues whose presence I didn't particularly enjoy. Especially I didn't have to take care of a handful of individuals who called regularly, demanded large chunks of my time and the conversation always centered about their problems or their needs.

In many ways, I could change and no longer do things the way I had done them for years. Having to pull away from ordinary life because of the fire gave me the opportunity to change. I was free. The past was behind me and it would stay behind me—if I chose to leave it there. I didn't have to allow those people to deplete my energies.

I know people who choose to remain in the past. For example, Frank's wife died of cancer and he deeply mourned her. He was Shirley's brother and they had no children, so we invited him to live with us. I don't think a day passed during the next three years when Frank didn't talk about the loss of his wife. "I hope you die before Shirley does," he often said to me. "I don't want you to have the pain I have to go through." Once he said that, he again told me of his deep loss.

Until he died, five years later, Frank never moved beyond the death of his wife. He chose to live in the past and recall the things they had done together.

More than anyone else, Frank helped me grasp how important it is to put the past into the past. I don't want to be chained to memories—even good ones. I want to live in the present.

But more than just pulling away from certain individuals, I had other things to put behind me. I could drag along painful memories of my own failures and shortcomings; or I could set a boundary and not allow those memories to intrude in the present.

That reminds me that God operates that way. His focus isn't on what used to be but on what is. For example, one time when Jesus spoke to the religious leaders about the resurrection, he said, "Haven't you ever read about this in the Scriptures? Long after Abraham, Isaac, and Jacob had died, God said, 'I am the God of Abraham, the God of Isaac, and the God of Jacob.' So he is the God of the living, not the dead" (Matt. 22:31-32).

We can focus on those things taken from us
or we can realize that loss can also bring freedom.

8

Facing Others' Problems

Eleanor emailed me and told me about a problem in her small group. One member had suffered the loss of a son, was bitter over the experience and took out her hostility on the others.

"I need your advice," she wrote, and gave me the details. The matter seemed too complex for an email reply, so I asked her to call me, which she did.

I asked a question or two, but mostly I let her talk. After she had mentioned her options, she again asked for advice.

Using different words, I repeated her options.

"I still don't know what to do," she said.

"Sure you do."

There was silence on the other end, and Eleanor finally said, "I guess I do. I needed you to give me permission."

She didn't mean that I had that kind of authority, but that she needed someone to affirm her decision and say, "That's exactly right." Because she was unsure of herself, Eleanor wasn't able to ask the question in a direct manner and perhaps wasn't even sure of the answer herself.

Sometimes I've done the same thing as Eleanor did. I've gone to someone and said, "I don't know what to do." I've asked for help and too often the other person has listened to my words but not to my heart.

That is, the other person has done exactly what I asked and given me advice. It's interesting that even though I wasn't conscious of the right answer and received counsel that wasn't right, I sensed it didn't fit. That situation is probably true for most of us.

When friends ask us to listen to their troubles and help them, that's rarely what they want. They want us to listen. They want us to care. They want us to feel their pain and their hurt. Friends don't usually need our advice; they do need us to listen.

Twenty years ago, Bryan McFarland poured out his pain to me for several minutes. When he paused, I said, "I really don't know how to help you."

Anger flashed in his eyes and he said, "Did I ask you to fix me?"

I don't remember my answer, but I can't forget his question. He wanted my understanding and my compassion. While I listened, I tried to figure out how to help him. I was absolutely wrong.

If I had kept my mouth shut, I would have helped him in the way he wanted. I could have shown him that I understood and that I cared. Here's another way to say it. I focused on myself and on what I could do for him; I forgot to focus on caring for him.

That wasn't my first offense, but it was the first time I became aware of my compulsion to heal someone. "Compulsion to heal" is a strong phrase, but deep within that's what I was trying to do. On an unconscious level, I sought for exactly the right word, the correct statement, or the perfect Bible verse to cure him. I wasn't focused on him.

I'll explain this in reverse. In the late 1990s, I reached a fork in the road of my career path. I had done nothing but ghostwrite for others for 10 years. I began to ask if that's what I wanted to do for the rest of my writing career. I wrote an email to five writer friends and explained my dilemma. I made a point of saying that I didn't want their guidance, but solicited only their prayers for God to speak to me.

I read my email three or four times to make sure I was clear. Before I stopped working that day, all of them had responded. They expressed their love and appreciated that I would contact them. I wish each of them had stopped with that.

All five writers—every recipient—offered "helpful advice." Although stated differently, each urged me to make changes and they were straightforward in the direction they felt I should take. They didn't give me bad advice; they gave me unneeded guidance.

They wanted to fix me, to relieve my anxiety and to set me straight. I appreciated their zealousness, but they disappointed me. As I wrote my email to them, I had come to the same conclusion that they urged, pleaded and begged me to consider. I already knew the answer but I still wasn't ready to take the step.

I could have said, "They told me exactly what I was already thinking." I could have. Instead, I wish they had read the entire email.

My five friends didn't want to listen or allow me to struggle with my own issues: They wanted to make me well and happy.

Too many of us don't want to feel uncomfortable or helpless, so we come up with answers and solutions to others' problems. We take them on (momentarily at least) as if they were our own.

Their responses helped me figure out what it means when people ask for help. My role is not to solve their problems. My role is to care about them while *they* solve their problems. It's also an excellent pedagogical and psychological principle. The more I put the burden on others to figure out their own solutions, the more I help them. I don't come across as brilliant or insightful, but then, I don't need to do that.

At times, all of us need direct guidance. We want input and we can usually figure out how to ask for it. All too often, however, we receive unwanted advice and the camera points to the other person and we're cut from the scene.

*Help me, God, to listen to the question and not rush in with
answers. You're the source of wisdom and insight. Help me
point others to you and allow you to speak. Forgive me, dear
Lord, for trying to take over the role of the Holy Spirit.
Amen.*

*My role is not to solve others' problems;
my role is to care about them while they solve their problems.*

Those Grace Builders

"Every church has at least one!" he said with a twinkle in his eyes. "And if you don't get enough there, you'll have them as neighbors or relatives."

He called them *grace builders*.

"God has a wonderful purpose in sending certain people your way. They force you to pray intensely, read your Bible more faithfully and teach you lessons about patience and longsuffering. Those folks will help you grow in spiritual grace."

I smiled at my old professor. He had listened to 20 minutes of my complaining about two people in my congregation who moaned about every decision I made.

"They seem to have one major function: God uses them to help you grow as rapidly as possible. In the long run, they do more for you than all the sweet folks in the church."

"If that's true," I said and laughed, "I'd rather grow a little more slowly."

"It doesn't work that way. God sends you enough grace builders to stop you from getting either proud or comfortable; he sends you enough of the sweet ones to keep you encouraged."

Over the years, I've had my share of grace builders. Immediately I think of Hal. The rotund chairman of the finance committee shouted louder when I tried to reason with him, and he usually got the decisions he wanted.

For days before any big decision came up on the church board, Hal visited other board members or called them on the phone. He arrived at meetings at least half an hour early and pulled officers to the side for private caucuses.

People listened to Hal because he worked hard for the church. If we wanted any job done, from mopping up rain leaks to patching a roof, Hal was on call. For the three years I was his pastor, I can say that he did innumerable tasks for the church; he also hurt the growth of the congregation.

The mention of Hal's name still evokes a few sad feelings for me, even though we've not been in the same church for more than two decades. Immediately I think of four words that describe him: Overbearing. Insensitive. Dogmatic. Dominating.

Hal often brought me to my knees in prayer. Differences with him forced me into much heart-searching about my own motives.

Hal was the first of many I encountered during my pastorate; but the biggest grace builders were three sisters.

"Since you came, Mr. Murphey, our church has lost some of its dignity," Agnes said as she served me tea from an ornate silver pot resting on a silver tray. With the next breath she asked, "Milk or sugar?"

"One lump of sugar, please," and I reached for the cup.

Her two sisters sat across the room from me. They said nothing but nodded every time Agnes spoke.

"We had such—such quiet dignity before you came. I don't want to hurt your feelings in telling you, but you call those noisy children to the front for a children's sermon. And they're so—so undisciplined. It disturbs the sanctity of the worship hour."

She smiled like an angel as she offered me a cookie from a silver plate.

"I'm sorry you feel that way," I said. "For me, children are important. I want them to feel part of the worship. Church isn't exclusively for older people."

"Yes," she said. Her lips smiled, but her eyes didn't. "But they also need to learn to be reverent in God's house. Why, they whisper as they go forward. And when you ask questions, they all yell out answers and—"

Agnes had other observations to make—quite a few. She summed it up by saying, "Now, we realize you've only been in the church a short time, but I wanted you to know how I felt about it."

"Thanks for being so open." I paused, foolishly hoping one of them would back down, but no one did. "I'm sorry you feel the way you do."

"You do understand." Her lower facial muscles smiled again.

"And I'm sorry you can't accept the way I do things," I said. I smiled, hoping it might lighten the atmosphere.

The two sisters turned their faces away from me.

As I left, Agnes made no attempt to return my smile; the two sisters shook their heads.

Depression weighted me down as I walked away. Was Agnes right? Had I been too adamant? Too judgmental toward her attitude?

"Lord, help me be more loving toward Agnes," I prayed, "and toward other people who disagree with me."

Now I remember that day and I can say, "Thanks, Agnes. You forced me into fervent prayer for the next few days. You became the best grace builder in my life at that time."

There have been others, and I meet them regularly.

Like Howard. When we meet, he pats me on the back and sounds friendly. The buddy-buddy type. He seems to make everything sound funny, even when he insults or ridicules me.

I don't feel persecuted. But I have enough sense to know when a person insults me even though hiding behind jokes and light-hearted humor.

And I can't forget Bob and Rita. They often told me, "You need more time to relax. Take off for a day or two and do nothing."

The first time Rita said those words and Bob followed with words of agreement, I beamed. *They cared. They cared about me.*

That is, unless *they* needed me. "I tried several times Friday to get you on the phone," Rita said Sunday morning. "I must have called five times." (That was before cell phones.)

"I spent the afternoon doing a few personal items I've wanted to get done for a couple of weeks," I replied.

"But *all day*? I mean, I kept trying to get hold of you."

Okay, Rita, I got your message: I can take off as much time as I want—except when you need me.

We all have our grace builders. Mine didn't show up only during my days as a pastor. They have the marvelous ability to find me no matter what I do or where I live.

And I have to admit they become the instruments of God—not because God calls them to behave as they do. They drive us to our knees. The grace builders help us mature and become stronger. We don't like them, but we *need* these folks to keep us moving ahead.

I don't like the grace builders in my life. I've tried to avoid them as much as possible. With others, I grit my teeth and face them.

I pause to think of the particular grace builders at work in my life. They're obnoxious. Self-centered. Opinionated. Demanding. Always disagreeable.

Without them I could accomplish more, get sidetracked less by annoying pettiness and feel better about life. *Or could I?* That's when I remind myself: *God uses these people in my life.*

And when some of these grace builders dominate a portion of my life, I find great comfort in Hebrews 12: "Be patient when you are being corrected! This is how God treats his children. Don't all parents correct their children? God corrects all his children, and if he doesn't correct you, then you don't really belong to him. . . . It is never fun to be corrected. In fact, at the time it is always painful. But if we learn to obey by being corrected, we will do right and live at peace" (Heb. 12:7-8,11, *CEV*).

In my struggles with grace builders, several things have become apparent to me.

First, I can't resolve all the conflicts. Life has a way of heaping one problem upon another. My growth takes place in the midst of those situations and because of those people.

Like Agnes. I saw her three times after that incident. Twice in the hospital (she had a heart condition), and once at the funeral of an elderly member of our congregation. She stopped attending our church and vowed to other church members never to return "as long as that man is there." (She kept her vow.)

I didn't try to pacify her. Perhaps I should have tried, but I sensed she would accept nothing less than capitulation from me. I saw no way to resolve our differences.

One day after a particularly painful experience with my supposed friend Howard, I said to myself, *Everybody didn't like Jesus either.*

That helped me deal with my own human limitations. I didn't have to be Superman, Solomon or the apostle Paul. I am Cec Murphey.

Another thing: I find solace in thinking that people like Howard, Agnes, Rita and Bob must have their own share of grace builders. (Yes, I smile as I think of that.) Surely the problematic people have other functions in life besides helping me grow.

In fact, I suspect that I'm the grace builder for several people.

Grace builders are the difficult people who upset us and force us to pray more fervently and grow more quickly.

Fixing Others

We hadn't seen Carol in the 20 years after I left the pastorate. In the decade that I had been her pastor, not once had I heard her compliment anyone or say a kind thing about others.

We met again at a funeral. Carol has been blind since birth, so my wife and I went over to where she stood by herself and said hello to her.

"Oh, yes, Shirley, you . . ." she said and talked about something my wife had supposedly said that hurt her feelings. That was nearly 30 years earlier, and she still carried it in her frontal lobe.

Her words shocked me. Perhaps I had been naïve, but I assumed that over that period of time she would have changed and become kinder and more considerate. I didn't say anything to her about it and the only thoughts that came to my mind would have been as harsh as the words she blurted out.

I shook my head as we walked away. "She hasn't changed, has she?" I said to Shirley.

On the drive home I thought about Carol and her attitude. Perhaps I had bought into the stereotype that the blind are kind, soft-spoken, gentle people instead of being human and fallible like anyone else. Mentally I reviewed harsh things she had said to me and to or about others in the church. *No,* I decided, *she hasn't changed.*

Recently, I thought of Carol again. "She has to be one of the most miserable people around," I said aloud. "She doesn't merely dislike people, she dislikes herself. Because she senses nothing good in herself, how could she believe anyone else would be good?"

Jesus said it this way: "A tree is identified by its fruit. If a tree is good, its fruit will be good. If a tree is bad, its fruit will be bad. . . . For whatever is in your heart determines what you say. A good person produces good things from the treasury of a good heart, and an evil person produces evil things from the treasury of an evil heart" (Matt. 12:33-35).

One day, I spoke with a friend about another person much like Carol—someone he knew slightly. On three or four occasions at church I had tried to be friendly and open with Mitch but he rebuffed me or insulted me. "Can you imagine all the negative energy there must be in him?" my friend said. "His mind must constantly focus on negative, self-critical thoughts. How could he like you when he can't even like himself?"

My friend was right. Despite that, both Mitch and Carol would be quick to say they believe in Jesus Christ. They are active church members and both serve among the congregation. Carol has perfect pitch in her left ear and plays the organ and piano beautifully. She can hear a note and tell you exactly what it is. Mitch is one of those people who is always at church to do the little tasks such as cleaning up after banquets or social activities. He's handy and has solved many minor emergencies.

They're talented and they serve, but they don't like people very much because they don't like themselves very much. For instance, on two occasions I tried to talk to Carol about music at the church. The first time I congratulated her because of a special version of a musical. "But [the baritone] sharped a B natural." She went on about the imperfections of the choir.

That time I thought she was merely being modest, so I smiled and thanked her again for the fine job she and the choir had done. "Anita is always too loud," she said adamantly.

"She probably thinks she's doing a solo instead of blending with the other voices."

I was a slow learner, so it took me a few times before I figured out her personality. That's when I began to grasp Jesus' words about what's on the inside. No matter who we are, our real personalities eventually come out.

The same with Mitch. As talented as he was, he constantly criticized others. Almost every week he verbally reported on what the custodian had failed to do. One time I said, "Don't you think he ever does anything right?"

"That's not the issue," he said. "The issue is what he neglects or does badly."

Poor Mitch. It was as if he felt his mission in life was to point out the weaknesses and failures of others. One day I thought, *Maybe that's his defense. If he attacks others, no one gets the opportunity to attack him. It's not that others would want to attack, but he probably wouldn't think that way. He probably assumes everyone is like him.*

In thinking of the Mitches and Carols in my life, I've come to a simple conclusion: When we don't like ourselves, we need to change others; when we like ourselves, we don't need to fix anyone.

As I learn to accept myself, I learn to accept others.

My Unacceptable Parts

I once taught a group of young adults, and I handed each a pen and a sheet of paper. I assured them that no one would see their responses.

"On one side of the paper, I want you to write five things you don't like about yourself."

"That's easy," one young man called out, and the others laughed.

They wrote quickly and within one minute all 23 had their answers.

"Turn your papers over. On the second side I want you to write five things you like about yourself."

They started to work on their responses. After a full minute, the young man who had spoken up earlier said, "This is hard."

I smiled and waited. After what seemed an appropriate time, I asked how many had filled out the first side with five answers. Every hand went up. "How many of you wrote five things you like about yourself?" About two-thirds of them raised their hands.

"Does it count if it's something you would like to be?"

After laughter I said, "Only if it's true now."

Other people have done this with varying results, but it proved to me what I'd suspected for a long time—and I think it may be especially true in Christian circles. We can tick off the negatives. Most of us remain conscious of our weaknesses and shortcomings, or what we assume are our negatives.

In our worship services, we tend to focus on sin and encourage people to examine their hearts. Some churches have a time in worship services called Confession of Sin, when people pray, often silently, as the worship leader directs them. Afterward, the leader follows with something called "Assurance of Pardon."

Christian theology constantly reminds us that all of us are sinners, and we have dozens of Bible verses to illustrate the point. But we don't do much in the church life to help people look at the positives in their personalities. Some would object that seeing the positives leads to pride and boasting.

Maybe they're correct. But somewhere between "God, be merciful to me a sinner" and "In Jesus Christ we are forgiven" wouldn't it be encouraging to have a segment called "Affirmation of God's People"?

We need affirmation—all of us do. And some of us receive it; others are so needy, they tell us how good or worthy they are so we'll have to affirm them. For years I kept a small sign on the corner of my desk:

> *You need 4 hugs a day for survival.*
> *You need 8 hugs a day for maintenance.*
> *You need 12 hugs a day for growth.*
>
> VIRGINIA SATIRE, AMERICAN AUTHOR AND PSYCHOTHERAPIST

Physical hugs or verbal hugs—both work—and we need them.

I make a point of this because of this aphorism: *I accept the unacceptable parts of myself.* The unacceptable may not be defeated or failed areas; they may also be the good parts—the talents and abilities that we refuse to recognize.

For example, when I was a pastor, I convened an annual Church Leader's Retreat. I invited elders as well as individuals within the congregation whom I considered emerging leaders.

During the first retreat, we made sure everyone knew everyone. Then I did a risky thing. I asked them to point to the most outstanding talent or gift they saw in the others. When Susan

Cothran's turn came, the word she heard was "administrator."

Her shocked expression told me she hadn't known she had that ability. She had been superintendent of the Sunday School, but she hadn't seen that as expressive of her ability (even though she did a superb job). We pointed her to something she had not accepted in herself: her administrative ability.

Too often we're afraid to acknowledge the good things about ourselves. We'd like them to be true, but to admit them seems as if we're bragging. However, if we don't admit them—and they're true—we're denying the grace of God at work in us. Part of our growth and a more intimate knowledge of God is to admit who we are. Have you ever wondered how difficult it must have been for Moses to write that he was the most humble man in the world (see Num. 12:3)? He did it because he realized he hadn't made himself humble. He merely admitted what God had already done in his life.

If we find part of ourselves unacceptable, how does God look at us? I think of it this way. God knows and has always known our failures, weaknesses and shortcomings, and the divine love accepts us as we are—as we are right now.

If there are parts of ourselves we haven't accepted, isn't it a way of saying we haven't fully received God's gifts to us? If we have ability that we can't, don't or won't acknowledge, we haven't fully appreciated God's gifts.

If our desire is to know ourselves so that we'll know God better, or the reverse, to understand God better, so we'll understand ourselves better, part of that desire needs to center on accepting *every* part of ourselves—the things we like and the things we dislike.

I accept the unacceptable parts of myself.

When I Suffer

What does it mean to be content? A Buddhist friend once said, "It's to be without desires." Maybe he was correct, but it didn't feel right to me. Besides, I find it difficult to think of trying to live without desires.

Furthermore, I'm not sure I'll ever be totally free of desires. And I find nothing in the Bible that speaks against desires or yearnings.

"For I have learned to be content whatever the circumstances" (Phil. 4:11, *NIV*). Paul wrote from a prison cell to the church at Philippi that he *learned* contentment. It wasn't a natural attribute; however, to want and not to receive is the area of pain.

For most of us, when we're unable to grasp what we yearn for, we feel like failures or rail at God for not giving us the desires of our heart.

When I think of thwarted desires, an Old Testament story in 1 Kings 21 intrigues me. King Ahab's palace was next to the vineyard of Naboth, and the king wanted that piece of land. He offered to buy it, but Naboth refused. In Israel the land came by inheritance, and the king couldn't simply take it away.

"So Ahab went home angry and sullen because of Naboth's answer. The king went to bed with his face to the wall and refused to eat!" (1 Kings 21:4). That was a non-clinical way to show Ahab's depression. But that's not the end of the story. Queen Jezebel talked to him and took over. She paid two men to accuse Naboth of blasphemy and used the Law of Moses to condemn him to death. Thus, Ahab could get out of bed and take over the piece of land.

The king's greed led Queen Jezebel into that despicable action. Or, we could say it was the king's discontent or strong desires that started the problem.

If I had to rank sins according to their evil content, I'd place discontent high on the list. In itself it's not so bad, but it's where being unsatisfied or unfulfilled can lead us. Discontent isn't about not having. Disgruntlement says much more, especially for those who profess faith in Jesus Christ.

If we yearn for what we don't have, we suffer and yearn for those things and think of them constantly. Instead of being desirable, they take on such importance and so consume our energies that they become necessities. "I have to own that," people say.

It's not wrong to want, and it's certainly not wrong to work for something we seek to achieve. But when we become heavily focused on a plot of ground, a magnificent house, the position of CEO or a million-dollar bank account, we've spoken against God's provisions for us.

If we believe another of my aphorisms, "Everything I am and everything I have come as gifts from God" (and I do), that statement encourages contentment. It doesn't stifle desire or stop us from trying to succeed in our careers. It does say that God has given us exactly what we need. If we can accept God's provision for now, and work faithfully without yearning or coveting, we're probably in a good place.

But if anything—a vineyard, a family or a job—becomes the unhealthy focus of our energies, we miss something important about our relationship with God. If, however, we start with what God has provided, and like the apostle learn contentment, we know we're in the right place. From there, God can take us forward.

First Kings 3 records a dream in which God appeared to King Solomon and asked, "What do you want? Ask, and I will give it to you!" (v. 5). The king said, "Give me an understanding heart so that I can govern your people well and know the difference between right and wrong" (v. 9).

The Bible says the answer pleased God because Solomon didn't ask for long life, wealth or the death of his enemies, so he promised Solomon a "wise and understanding heart" (v. 12). "And I will give you what you did not ask for—riches and fame" (v. 13).

That seems like the best spiritual principle: The more I grasp my relationship with God and express my thanks, the more abundantly God provides for me.

I'll give an example. One of my late writer friends published 31 books before he died. He told me, "I pray for every one of them to sell a million copies." I see nothing wrong with that, but it was what followed. He focused his energies on becoming the best-selling writer in the Christian publishing world. He did everything he could to make better deals, get higher royalties and make certain his books were prominently displayed in stores. It seemed like an obsession to me.

And he suffered when someone he heard about wrote a book that sold more copies. One time he referred to a best-selling author and said, "I'm a better writer than he is." Another time he said, "I work harder at my writing than he does and I deserve my sales."

I learned from watching him, and it was a negative lesson that he taught me. It's all right to want; it's all right to pray; but when we put our desires first in our lives, and we don't get them, we suffer. We feel resentment, depression and perhaps even anger.

When I yearn for what I don't have, I suffer;
when I accept what God has given me, I am content.

Do You Love Me?

I've figured out the worst question children ask their parents: "Do you love me?"

Why is that such a terrible question? It's one no child should ever have to ask.

If people love me, I usually know. They will have ways to show me. Some show in words, some by their actions; but genuine love always, always finds some method of expression.

As a child, I didn't feel loved. When I was six years old, I said to my mother, "You love Mel more than you do me." Mel was my younger brother and obviously our parents' favorite. The other six of us knew that, but Mom wouldn't ever admit it.

"I love all of you the same," she said.

That was the most unsatisfying answer she could have given me. How can anyone love seven children the same way? Even at my young age, I knew that was impossible. I tried to figure out how she could do that, and I asked her what she meant.

"I love all of you the same," she said again and walked away.

She used the word "love," but the word didn't make me feel loved.

Most people yearn to hear someone say, "I love you" or "I care about you." None of us ever gets enough love or affirmation. Some boldly ask for assurance, but most of us sulk in private.

I understand the need to feel loved, but it's not only because of my childhood. I also understand this especially in my former role as a pastor. I began to grasp it in high school but I didn't understand it for at least 30 years later.

Often I befriended someone, and I had a proclivity toward the outsiders and those shunned by others. I remember homely and slightly retarded Laura Bish in third grade. I was the only child in the class who gave her a valentine. Gene Walenz had a glass eye as a result of childhood cancer. A group of us gathered in booths at a restaurant before school every morning. When I saw Gene alone for the second morning, I invited him to join our group and he became one of us.

I'm not pointing to my good deeds to show how wonderful I am, but people like Gene (and others) later said, "You're my best friend." I heard that often in high school and even more frequently in college. During my pastoral days, the message came regularly. After I left the pastorate and taught in conferences and preached in churches, people I met one time and corresponded with later said the same thing.

"How could that be?" I often asked.

I finally figured it out with David Morgan. One day he said to me (or I said to him—we can never remember which of us said it), "You were everybody's best friend but you never had a best friend."

That's when the insight came. I expressed love—perhaps not the word "love," but in some way I demonstrated the kind of expression some people needed. I assume they had no one who showered them with attention, who loved or accepted them as they were without laying demands on them.

I didn't do it perfectly, and I don't think of myself as some kind of messianic figure. But I think I demonstrated—in small, intangible ways—the message they yearned to hear. For some of them, I took on the role of best friend.

Was I the best friend because I was the first (or the only) one to encourage, to uplift, to speak kindly? Perhaps. But it also speaks of the paucity of their relationship.

This much I know: If I care about someone, I'll find a way to express my feelings. Furthermore, if I do it well, those others will know I love them even if I don't use words.

Perhaps that's the biggest challenge for us. It's not only to love but also to find ways to express Jesus' love to hurting, broken people. We can do it. It may take effort and we might have to learn new ways to behave—but we can do it.

If we love others, we will find ways to express our feelings.

14

Remembering and Forgetting

I returned to Kenya, East Africa, about a decade after I left. From Nairobi, I drove upcountry—into the bush—an area near Lake Victoria. It was still primitive, and another four years would pass before they had electricity and telephones.

On my second day upcountry, we held a worship service at a place called Migori, and we later met in the pastor's house—a one-room structure with mud walls and a thatch roof.

Seven or eight pastors gathered around a table with me for a meal. During the conversation, Nathaniel turned to me and asked, "Do you remember when you . . . ?"

One by one they began asking me if I remembered things such as being awakened at two o'clock in the morning and rushing a wife to the hospital who was having trouble delivering her baby. Another pastor mentioned a time when he went through financial difficulty and I gave him money to pay his college tuition. One man recalled a time when I had helped him through a deep spiritual issue.

As I listened to their "Do you remember when . . . ?" stories, I honestly couldn't remember most of the incidents they mentioned. I kept shaking my head and saying, "I don't remember."

But I remembered many kind things they did for me. Erastus helped me learn the Luo language; Henry once traveled more than 20 miles on his motorcycle, over bad roads, to find me, because he feared our car had broken down. It had and he gave me a ride back to our mission compound. My list of good things they had done for me was extensive—interrupted only by their reminding me of something I had done for them.

Finally, Blasio, who had been to school eight years at most, looked at me and his brown eyes lit up suddenly as he said, "Ah, that is good."

Then Blasio made one of the most profound statements I've ever heard. Translated into English, it goes like this: "He who gives must never remember; he who receives must never forget."

Years later, I still remember those words. I want to have a poor memory when it comes to what I've done for others. If our attitude is right, we give from one primary motivation— we give as *a gift to God*. And it can be that when we remind ourselves that God has freely given us all things, we show our appreciation by responding to God's love through our generous giving.

It's not enough to give, however; we also need to forget our good deeds. Some of the worst giving I've seen involves people who give to others and later remind them of their gift. I've been guilty of that a few times. Jesus taught the opposite: "When you give alms, do not let your left hand know what your right hand is doing" (Matt. 6:3, *RSV*).

Best of all, God gives to us in the same measure that we give to others. Thus, as we give freely to God, God doesn't withhold from us.

Recently, I went through my business accounts for the past three years. I had to justify my contributions on my taxes. I particularly noticed a woman for whom I had provided a scholarship to a conference. She's someone I've recently gotten to know well.

I laughed when I read her name. I didn't remember helping her. "That's so wonderful, Lord!" I yelled. "I didn't remember!"

That's how I want to do all my giving—to give freely and realize that my gifts are to God. My desire is to give so freely that
I'll never be able to recall any charitable act.

*God, help me remember others' acts of kindness to me; enable
me to forget my acts of kindness to others.*

My Negative Feelings

I'm an emotional person and try to stay in touch with my feelings. I've met too many people, especially in the church, who frown on feelings. They prefer to analyze, ponder and make rational decisions based on an exhaustive amount of information.

I don't have any problem with their way of making decisions and living their lifestyles, but I don't want that imposed on me. I tend to make my decisions from my gut. I prefer to say, "I listen to my intuitive voice."

Most of the time that works well for me. I like to be open to people; I'm affectionate, and people tell me I'm warm. One reason I've done well as a ghostwriter/collaborator is that I'm in touch with my own feelings and I can sense how others feel. I'm comfortable talking about my emotions and I invite others to open up to me.

I like that, but there's a negative side to people like me.

We trust our feelings—which isn't wrong—especially when we feel on top or joyful. But some days we don't feel good about ourselves or we don't feel positive and upbeat.

Over the years I've realized how easy it is to confuse feelings with reality. Although I know the difference, sometimes my heart overrules my head. I haven't fully won this battle, although I wish I could say I have.

I'll explain it this way. When I work on a book project—and it could be any task I have to do—at some point the doubts intrude. For example, when I worked on a different part of this book, negative thoughts rushed through my brain:

· This is worthless.
· Who wants to read this tripe?
· Why are you wasting your time on this junk?
· Everybody knows this simplistic stuff.
· Why add more garbage to the world?

In those times I have to pull back, and I have one sentence I repeat that helps me fight those intrusive, depressing thoughts: "My negative feelings are emotions; they are not reality." Most of the time after I've said those words two or three times, I'm all right again. But not always.

When the sentence hasn't been enough, I pause and ask myself, "What's going on that makes me feel this way?" (I often talk aloud to myself.) The first time I asked, it didn't take long before I remembered a rejection I had received from a publishing house only the day before. The editor didn't say I wrote badly. Her letter was vague; but I thought, *She probably hates my writing*. That rejection was like a dollop of poison that threatened my entire day. *I must be lousy or she would have joyfully accepted it.*

I don't always get answers like that. Sometimes I can't discern a reason. But I have learned one thing in the process: The more deeply I care about something, the more I have to pay attention to my emotions.

For instance, I've had an extremely difficult time in writing this book. It's taken me much longer than it usually does for a book of this size. I know the reason: It's because I decided to bare my soul, and my biggest fear is that people will scoff or laugh at my shallowness. More than in anything I've written before, I'm giving myself as fully as I know how and putting my heart on this page. And it's all I have to offer.

"My negative feelings are emotions; they are not reality." I had to repeat those words to myself as soon as I wrote the words above.

This isn't all bad. I've begun to appreciate the censorious voice as my protector. It's like the guard who stands at the palace gate. He's always on duty and his responsibility is to protect me from hurt, rejection or humiliation. He tries to shield me from danger. I need him, because the deeper I dig into myself, the more my emotions cry out, "Don't!" And the best way isn't just to say no, but to make me feel I'm writing bilge, junk or gunk.

I decided I wanted to write this book anyway. So, on almost every page, I have to repeat those soothing words.

My negative feelings are emotions;
my negative feelings are not reality.

16

Trusting Others

Eighteen years ago, I discovered a wonderful secret about relationships with others. I call it a secret because it remained hidden to me for an extremely long time.

A member of my Sunday School class called me and asked, "May I come and see you? I have to talk to somebody." I suggested he talk to the pastor, but he said, "I feel closer to you." I told Mark to come over.

His story isn't important to relate here, but he faced severe personal problems in his career. "They've decided to close our office and move everything to Dallas. They didn't even give me the option of going." Mark was the head of his department.

They did offer him a nice separation package that amounted to eight months of salary and insurance—a month for each year he had been with the company. Mark was devastated that he had no job and didn't know what to do. He worked in a highly specialized industry and there weren't many similar positions open to him. He told me about the angry feelings he felt toward his superiors and that he had trusted them. They had all but promised to have a good position for him with the Dallas office.

He held his head in his hands and cried.

I had no idea what to say to him, but after several minutes of silence I told him about the time I faced a somewhat similar situation. "Outwardly, I was fine," I said, "but inwardly the stress was too much. I ended up in the hospital with ulcers."

Mark stared at me. "You? You worried? You folded under stress?"

After I admitted that, he opened up even more and told me about his fuming response. "I had to leave the office or I feel I would have punched my boss in the face."

"I know how that feels." I told him of a time in Africa when I became that enraged over something another missionary had done. The man I wanted to punch out wasn't home. "It's probably just as well," I said. "He was my size but a lot stronger. He would have decked me."

Mark slowly shook his head in unbelief and then he smiled. That's when things changed. Mark pulled out his handkerchief and wiped away his tears. He hugged me and thanked me for telling him. Minutes later he opened up about other things in his life, including a short-lived affair with a woman in his office. No one else knew, and the woman had left more than a year earlier. But he spoke of his guilt. "I never told my wife, and it eats at me; but if I tell her, I feel she'll never trust me again."

I didn't advise Mark because that was between God and Mark, but I did ask, "Why did you decide to tell me about the affair?"

"Because I trust you. I've always liked you and I knew you would listen; but when you told me about how badly you handled a few situations, I saw a new side of you. I've known you were a strong Christian, but I didn't realize that you faced hardships and tough times like I do."

He smiled. "I didn't know you could get boiling mad."

Mark shocked me, but I got the message. I opened up to him and he was able to open up to me. That's probably obvious; but that wasn't the secret. The secret was that I opened up because I could. I opened up to him because I trusted myself enough to know that it was all right.

When I told Mark my embarrassing story about anger, I didn't worry about his reaction or whether he'd despise me for being weak. I was secure enough that I could tell him and not hold back—regardless of his reaction. The secret was because I honestly felt forgiven and I could use my mistakes to understand others who failed. I trusted myself to talk freely, and Mark responded by trusting me.

It's wonderful when relationships work that way.

When I trust myself enough to be myself,
others can respond by trusting me.

17

New Places, Old Problems

An old story says that a man visited a city, thinking it might be a good place to live. He talked to the head of the chamber of commerce. "What kind of people live here?"

"What kind of people do you live with now?"

"Oh, a lot of negative types, always complaining, and never happy."

"You'll find this city is the same way," the man said.

The point of the story is that we carry our problems with us. We may move to a new city or a new country. The location changes; the problems don't. They may come in different forms, but they're essentially the same issues.

As obvious as it is, it took me a long time to understand that. When we lived in Africa, I realized that I had a serious problem with anger. An older missionary said, "This country brings out the best in the people and it also brings out the worst." I believed him.

Because I believed him, I was able to pacify my guilt and say that it was because of living in a strange land and having to learn different customs and new languages. Those things were true, but I wasn't ready to admit that the situation could only bring out what was already inside me.

About two years after our return to the United States, I realized I still had a bad temper. I have one of those quick-to-explode-and-quick-to-burn-out temperaments. Within minutes

I'm usually over my anger, but I leave carnage behind and hurt feelings.

My problem wasn't the culture or the city where we lived. My problem was Cec Murphey. I had issues, some of them severe, that I needed to face but didn't want to admit to them. Sometimes my anger focused on the way others behaved; sometimes I became irate over situations I didn't like. I had all kinds of categories and causes in which I could catalog everything.

But one day I faced it: My anger was a serious problem and it had been with me as far back as I could remember—and perhaps before I could remember. I don't know the cause, and hunting for it isn't worthwhile. I think most of it was learned because my temperament was much like my father's. When he was upset, it was as if a tidal wave had hit the house, rushed through it and then was almost immediately gone.

Even if it is true that I learned my behavior by watching my dad (or that I had inherited his temperament), it still didn't excuse me. I had to face my own issues, and the answer seemed quite simple. I expected life to function in a particular way. When everything didn't work as I anticipated, I was upset.

I didn't experience a miraculous healing or an instantaneous deliverance. Anger still sneaks up on me. More and more frequently, I become aware of its surreptitious approach and I cry out for help.

Sometimes I face my anger only after the fact and have to cry out, "Forgive me, Lord Jesus." But I serve a merciful God who stays with me, even when I fail. Each time I fail, I hear myself saying, "Next time? Dear Lord, let there not be a next time."

Our problems arise out of who we are.
Although they come in different forms,
the same problems find us no matter where we run.

Helping the Guilty

"Every Sunday I felt guilty when I entered the church building, and I felt even more guilty when I left." A man said that to me about his former church. For nearly 15 years he had attended the same church.

I don't remember most of his words, but one sentence stood out: "No matter how hard I tried all week to be a good Christian, when I listened to the sermon the minister found a way to make me feel guilty."

Because I knew the pastor, I felt certain he didn't intentionally preach guilt and condemnation. However, like many believers in the business world or in the neighborhood, many of us are adept at laying guilt on others or accepting guilt when it's not intended.

I understand guilt, and I grew up with it. I often say that as a child I ate it three times a day. No matter what I did, I never pleased my father. He was excellent at pointing out my defects or yelling at me for doing something wrong. The best I ever received from him was silence. It wasn't approval, but at least it wasn't condemnation.

After the criticism came the brief-but-blaming lectures and angry statements on how I should have done something different. I assume that's a strong reason I try to move in the other direction. I like to affirm others. I like to shower them with the deserved praise I didn't receive as a child.

I've learned one significant lesson from coping with my own culpability: Guilty people don't need a theology lesson on how to feel more guilty; they need assurance of God's love and acceptance.

Even as a child, when I had done something wrong, I knew it. Shame and self-reproach filled my heart. Neither of my parents ever said, "It's all right, but don't do it again. You were wrong, but we love you." My childhood world seemed to consist in not being culpable, or hiding my wrongdoing so my parents wouldn't find out I was the perpetrator.

Here's something else I figured out from my home environment: If I could make someone else feel ashamed, I could feel superior. If she did something wrong, it meant I must have done something good. If he failed in a situation, then I probably succeeded in what I did. Pointing the blame finger at someone is a self-protective device so we don't have to point to ourselves.

But what if we reversed that kind of thinking and began not blaming or inducing guilt? What if we decided to make others feel good about themselves and encouraged them to do only their best? Blaming works fine because people often recognize their faults; affirmation works even better because people can rise above their shortcomings.

What if we focused on the hurting person—the one who had failed—and in doing so we could look at life through those sorrowful eyes? What if we realized that we're prone to the same failures? What if we admitted that by encouraging them, we were also encouraging ourselves?

I believe it works that way. The more I nudge others to rise above their shame, guilt, humiliation or feelings of inadequacy, the more I pull myself up. That's how life operates: In helping others, we help ourselves.

We may not fight the same battles, but we all face skirmishes and struggles. One woman speaks first and thinks later. Another takes so long pondering that she actually hurts those who want a kind or affirming word. A man says, "Of course I like what she does. If I didn't, I'd tell her." It doesn't occur to him that silence doesn't mean praise.

When I'm wrong—and I become aware of it—please, please don't tell me I'm wrong, that I've sinned, goofed, failed or defaulted. I probably already know. Here's what you can do: You can say, "I'm sorry you messed up, but I love you. And I know that God loves you more than I do and forgave you long, long ago when Jesus died for your failures."

I'm determined to reach out to the guilty, not to expose them but to help them tear off the garments of self-deprecation and put on clothes of self-appreciation.

God, help me lift up the fallen instead of treading on their
backs and pushing them further into shame or failure.
Remind me they don't need lectures or theological
explanations. They need your love and your compassion and
I want to be the one who delivers that in person.

Guilty people don't need a theology lesson on how
to feel more guilty; guilty people need assurance of God's
love and acceptance.

All that Silence

I want to tell you two stories. In the first, I listened to a lecture in which the man presented a strong case for an ethical issue. It was a matter on which the Bible makes no direct statement.

As he spoke, he did what we call proof-texting. He cited Bible verses that, taken out of their literary context, seemed to support his position. What he said wasn't what I'd categorize as grave errors. Although I agreed with his position, I thought he could have made a better presentation. Three times I thought of corrective statements that would have made his presentation stronger and more acceptable. I could have given him biblical analogies as well as a few more logical statements.

At the end of his lecture, he asked for questions, and a few people raised their hands. They seemed to agree with him and sought only clarification on minor points.

I said nothing.

My second story is similar to the first, but I reacted differently. I visited an adult Sunday School class. I didn't agree with the woman teacher, but I thought, *Maybe she's right. Does it make any difference?* I asked myself and decided that it probably didn't matter. She was intelligent and had obviously studied the subject at length. I listened to her for the entire 45 minutes. When she asked for questions, two people raised their hands.

I remained silent.

What's the difference between the two stories? In the first, I was critical (that's easier to say than to admit I felt judgmental, smug or superior). A dozen thoughts raced through my mind but I chose not to argue. I kept quiet rather than be confrontational or controversial.

When I remained silent in the second story, however, it wasn't because I agreed. I sensed that it wasn't an important issue. But more than that, I listened with an open mind. I didn't feel smarter, wiser or more knowledgeable. Although I remained aware of differences with the teacher, I formed no critical thoughts.

I want to be clear: We need to speak up when it comes to principles and values we hold dear. That's not my point here. Too often I've disapproved and sometimes spoken disparagingly when another person didn't agree with me. Because I believed something, that seemed reason enough to want (at times even insist) that the other had to be mistaken. I wouldn't have said it aloud, but in those situations I felt I was a little brighter or better informed.

I've concluded that to remain silent is the more loving way. One quality of the highest form of biblical love (Greek, *agape*) is to accept others' opinions uncritically. I translate *agape* love as active caring.

If I actively care, can't I accept another's viewpoint being as valid as mine? To love others doesn't send me on a divine mission to correct their thinking or their theology. I don't have to decide on the correctness of their attitude.

In the Bible, Paul writes, "Knowledge puffs up, but love builds up" (1 Cor. 8:1, *NRSV*). Maybe I'm beginning to grasp what *agape* truly means.

> *If I love you, and I think you're mistaken, it's all right;*
> *if I don't love you, and I think you're mistaken,*
> *I'll either reject you or try to fix you.*
> *It's easier to love you.*

Being Lovable

Church members hear a different sermon every week, and the leaders have 66 biblical books from which to choose passages on which to base their messages. Although they have hundreds of things to talk about, most sermons would fit into a dozen categories. Love, eternity, punishment, justice and forgiveness are a few of them. And probably the most preached theme in the New Testament is about love. God loves us—and we find that theme all the way from John 3:16 to the letters of Paul and Peter.

So here's my question: If God's love for us is *the* core message and possibly the most proclaimed message in the New Testament, why don't all God's people feel loved? Why do so many say the right words about being loved, sing the hymns and choruses, but don't feel loved?

Maybe because it's preached so often that the theme of love no longer holds the excitement of the good news, *euangelion,* the Greek word usually translated as "gospel."

That's possible. Another reason that occurs to me is that we don't proclaim the love of God clearly. That is, we tend to tie it up with something else, such as our obedience, being good, praying, giving or forgiving.

As long as we hear, "God loves you and . . ." or "God loves you but . . ." we won't get it. I'm not trying to blame preachers, Sunday School teachers or church elders.

For me the problem is that God's love for us goes contrary to life. For example, when I was pastor at a suburban Atlanta church for 10 years, most people there liked me. That's not meant to be boastful, only factual (and there were always a few who didn't like me and would never like me).

Why did they like me? Let's assume they liked my preaching, but I think it was more than that. I spent time with members. I visited their homes before they joined, and I came around whenever they needed me. Before and after worship services I walked among the congregation. I assume most pastors do about what I did, so that's nothing unusual.

So why wouldn't they like me—maybe even love me? I worked hard and I reached out to them. Did you read the two previous sentences? I *earned* a good relationship with them. In many cases it was love and respect I received from others. For some it may have been merely appreciation. Regardless, I worked hard and I earned it.

That's how our society operates. We're paid for our services in money, respect or love. We don't have many opportunities to feel loved just for being who we are. If we're truly blessed, we feel that our spouse and our parents love us, perhaps our siblings and possibly a few of our co-workers. But those who feel this way are the minority, and some people never sense they're loved.

For years I transferred the way human relationships are to my relationship with God. I would have denied it, but deep within, I think I worked zealously for God so God would love me more.

It took me years to realize that God created me lovable and I didn't have to become lovable. Divine love reaches down to me and to all of us and says, "I created you and I love you." The Bible verse that speaks most clearly to me is a message given to Israel before they entered the new land: "The LORD did not set his heart on you and choose you because you were more numerous than other nations. . . . Rather, it was simply that the LORD loves you" (Deut. 7:7-8).

The point is that God provided no reason or explanation for loving them. God loves us simply because he loves us. That means we do nothing to increase love toward ourselves. Disobedience may result in punishment, but the penalty is really a demonstration of faithful love.

Why is it so hard to know I'm loved? One day I asked that question and I'm not sure I received an answer, but I had a satisfying thought. It's hard for many of us to believe in miracles or to accept anything that doesn't conform to the patterns of nature. Maybe that's how God's love also works.

Lord, help me to realize I don't have to become lovable;
you created me lovable.

God's Love for Me

This may not be rational, but if I worked hard, I honestly thought I could make God love me more. I didn't say those words aloud and would never have admitted I felt that way. But deep, deep within, that's exactly my attitude.

I could blame that on my childhood, when I was never able to please my father. I spent many of my adult years trying to please Dad, and that was even after he died. I suppose for me, it was some kind of transference of my understanding of my earthly father, and I laid it on my heavenly Father. I'll even say I believe that's what most of us do. We have some kind of tangled hardwiring in our brains that transfers our earthly image of our father to our heavenly Father.

One of the first sermons I heard after I became a believer was about the fatherhood of God and the love God had for me. That sermon meant a great deal to me and was the beginning of my distinguishing between my two fathers. It still took a long time to separate them, but it was the beginning.

But beyond realizing that God loved me, I pulled along things from childhood. I wasn't my dad's favorite. Mel, the special one, could ask for anything and get it—and the rest of us knew that. If I asked for anything, I rarely received it.

The few times I asked for and received what I wanted from Dad was when I begged repeatedly and he finally gave in. After I became a believer, that was the way I related to God. My heavenly Father didn't give freely, and I had to importune (a nicer word than "beg") until I felt assured of a positive response.

Along with that, because I didn't feel Dad loved me, I spent an inordinate amount of energy trying to prove to him that I was worth loving. I did it by achieving good grades and succeeding in my work.

On an unconscious level, that's how I related to God. If I wanted anything, I had to prove to God that I needed something and was worthy of receiving it. I often opened my spiritual résumé and pleaded.

- "I teach Sunday School every week."
- "I'm head of the early morning ushering program."
- "I give generously to our church."
- "I give to other charitable groups."
- "I help other writers."

It took a long time for me to realize that God loves me and wants to bless my life, and not because of anything I've done or would do. It took years before I realized I couldn't do anything to force God to love me more. Because God's love is everlasting and he has loved me from all eternity, how could it possibly increase? How could I find any more favor with God? What I had to learn was that the generous, ever-loving God was already reaching out to me with unsearchable, inexpressible love. I'm not the center of the world, but I'm the center of God's love. God's provisions are based on unconditional love, not on my faithfulness.

All this is to say that I'll never be able to make God love me more than he does. It's impossible because he already loves me perfectly.

*It's impossible for God to love me more tomorrow
than he loves me today.*

Our Weak Wills

I had come for a physical and sat in Dr. Morgan's waiting room. A few minutes later, an obese man came out of the office with the doctor. I heard only the end of their conversation, but apparently Dr. Morgan had put his patient on a strict diet and the man hadn't lost any weight.

"I try, doc, honest I do," he said, "but I guess my will is too weak."

By then they had passed me so I didn't hear the rest. But the man's statement struck me because I had talked to God that way. I'm not overweight but I have my own bag of problems. Sometimes I've been mean-spirited or jealous, or I've gossiped about someone. And later (or sometimes immediately) I feel convicted. I know better.

I used to berate myself by saying, "I've been a Christian all these years and I still . . ." But the excuse I used more often sounded like the obese man's feeble words. "My will is too weak."

It sounds a little like the words of Paul in Romans 7:14-24 where he says, in effect, "I know all the right things to do and I end up doing the opposite." He refers to an inner war. One part of him wants to obey God, and the other doesn't. After he struggles over the question, he finally cries out, "Oh, what a miserable person I am! Who will free me from this life that is dominated by sin and death?" (7:24).

Many times I used Paul's weakness account as an excuse. I reminded myself that we're all sinners and will never be free from the taint of sin.

But one time God pulled me up short. I had really told off a friend with strong and loud words. He had been wrong and I had overreacted. Later, I apologized to him and we straightened it out.

As I walked away, however, I asked God to forgive me. "Forgive me," I prayed, "my will is so weak."

I don't know if this was God's voice, but I knew it was correct. The inner voice whispered, "No, your will is too strong."

At first those words confused me. If I had such a strong will, why didn't I fully follow Jesus' commands? I finally figured out that other desires, often hidden ones, dominated my life. At that moment, I wanted something more than I wanted to obey the Lord.

Here's an illustration. I know that I need to love others and treat them the same way I want to be treated. That's the golden rule. At the same time, I have such an overwhelming need to be accepted, to be important or to feel worthwhile, even though I'm not usually aware of those needs. My inner desire for approval will supersede my aspiration to serve others.

Or dieting is another good illustration. No diet works long because it's usually based on some form of deprivation—what people can't eat. Eventually, most food restrictors will revolt and eat not only the forbidden foods but also even gorge on them. I don't know all the reasons most dieters fail in their task, but I'm sure it's because they have a deeply hidden need that's stronger than their yearning to lose weight.

Here's an example that helped me understand. When I was a pastor, Elsie was one of our most active members, and she was overweight. She often came to me to talk. One time she told me she had been raped when she was 14, at a time when she had barely developed physically. She showed me a picture of herself at that age and she was incredibly beautiful. "I thought I was raped because I was so beautiful; and if I was overweight, no one would bother me again." She said she hadn't been aware of that until she became a member of a group of women who opened up to each other about their weight issues.

That didn't resolve the issue for a woman in her late thirties, but at least she had begun to realize why she tried (and failed) every popular diet.

Losing weight. Maintaining an exercise program. Regularly reading the Bible. Praying daily. Attending church. Organizing your closet. Painting the guest room. The problem or issue doesn't matter, but the rule is simple: The greater need will always overpower the weaker.

I want my will to be surrendered to God so that pleasing my heavenly Father becomes the strongest, most earnest desire in my life, and at every moment.

> *"Forgive me," I prayed, "my will is so weak."*
> *God whispered, "No, your will is too strong."*

23

Among the Imperfect

During my Navy enlistment I worked under a female officer named Mary Ann. She worked hard, and our department always finished our work on time and often early. She demanded our best and wouldn't settle for less.

I liked that but I had one problem with Mary Ann—although I never told her. She was a perfectionist, an obsessive perfectionist. She did everything exactly right, and nothing left our office without her checking and rechecking and even initialing the final paper.

Mary Ann herself rarely made a mistake. When someone pointed out an error, she immediately went into denial and cover-up mode (as I saw it). Whenever possible she passed on the blame to someone with a lower rating. Twice I had to face the ire of our lieutenant because of a few minor mistakes that I hadn't made even though Mary Ann blamed me for them. The first time, I tried to protest, but it didn't do any good. I decided it was wiser if I silently listened, said, "Yes, sir," and went back to work.

In my two years of working under Mary Ann, my admiration and respect for her tumbled because she couldn't admit to human failure. She had to be infallible. Not once did I ever hear her say, "I'm sorry," or "I was wrong," even after someone actually showed her where she had miscalculated or goofed.

Five of us worked directly under her, and the murmuring went on behind her back constantly. "If only she didn't try so hard to be perfect," one of my co-workers said. The more Mary Ann insisted on being correct, the more we disliked her. In time, none of us appreciated her good qualities, and we probably saw her in worse light than she deserved.

I write all this because, at age 19, I learned an invaluable lesson. I decided I wanted to admit to my failures (even though it's not always easy) because people will overlook honest apologies. Admitting failure made me human in others' eyes, and I felt others appreciated me for being honest. Mary Ann was one of the reasons I decided to show the world that I'm an imperfect human being. When I try to show them I'm perfect, they see me as being even more flawed than I am.

Isn't it amazing how human nature works? If we're able to face our shortcomings and failures, people accept us and respect us for our openness. If we try to hide, deny or ignore, they turn from us.

God doesn't work like that, but there's a spiritual principle here. When I openly admit to God and to myself that I've failed, I become more accepting of myself, and that translates to my accepting others as they are. I think God smiles on me for that.

Don't we learn this lesson from King David? As imperfect as he was—and he had many flaws—he clearly won the favor of God. I can only assume it was because he was quick to repent and ask forgiveness. He didn't excuse himself or point to Bathsheba, as Adam did when he blamed Eve and said, "She gave me the fruit to eat."

Later, David wrote in Psalm 51:4, "Against you, and you alone, have I sinned." By that he meant that sin or wrongdoing hurts others but, ultimately, all failure points to our relationship with our loving Creator.

I've seen this principle with politicians, sports figures and church leaders. The first reaction of most of them is to deny any wrongdoing, but their failures seem to come out and get publicized far more than they would have otherwise. But if they say, as a few have done, "I was wrong," people forgive them and the transgression rarely comes up again. We seem to have an inborn need to ferret out the wrongdoers or the imperfect. And when we find out things they try to hide, we tend to overlook the good things in their lives because we're focused on their shortcomings.

I prefer to tell about my failures. I want to show the world that I'm an imperfect human being.

God, as I cry out in my imperfection, let me not
fear rejection by others. Instead, enable me to open
myself fully to you and to others.

When I try to show others that I'm perfect,
they see me as less perfect than I am.

24

Thoughtless People

Twice I tried to talk with the little girl, who was perhaps nine years old. She sat next to me at a dinner party and was one of the four children among more than 30 adults. I'd call her remarks rude or snide. After the second time, I shook my head and started to turn away.

"I don't have to be nice," she said. "That's what my mama has to do."

I didn't answer. I was too shocked to form a response for her but I thought about her words a great deal. Her attitude was extremely arrogant but different only in degree from many undisciplined youngsters.

Our children are sometimes thoughtless and unkind. But then, so are we. We wouldn't call ourselves thoughtless—but then, isn't that what the word means? It implies being unaware and not thinking about our behavior.

Kids act that way far too often. I wonder where they learned such behavior. I assume they learned it by observing others, probably their parents, as well as their peers. They behave rudely because they're not corrected or disciplined.

Because we love them, it's easy to excuse our children for being thoughtless or careless. We don't want to see their shortcomings. I wonder if God reacts the same way to his children.

I decided that God doesn't let us alone because we're ignorant, uninformed or don't know any better. Instead I like the admonition from the book of Hebrews, quoting from Proverbs: "My child, don't make light of the LORD's discipline, and don't give up when he corrects you. For the LORD disciplines those he loves, and he punishes each one he accepts as his child. As you endure this divine discipline, remember that God is treating you as his own children" (Heb. 12:5-7).

Too often things go wrong for us and we see it as punishment (and it may be just that). But sometimes it truly is the loving swat of divine discipline. We tend to behave like children who scream, protest and yell. Instead of pleading, "Help me know what I did wrong," our tendency is to push away all responsibility for the deed or to call life unfair. Among some Christians, their favorite saying goes, "The devil is really after me today."

What if it's God who tracks us down? Maybe it's the disciplining hand of a loving God who says, "I love you too much to let you get away with your unacceptable behavior."

When things go wrong, instead of seeing it as punishment, what if we prayed, "Help me learn from this. Help me see where I've been wrong"? Of course, some people would rather find other causes or contributing factors than to open themselves to God's tender-but-painful probing.

I don't doubt the spiritual forces of evil or the existence of the devil. It's that I believe more in a sovereign God who holds my hand and rebukes me when I'm wrong. And sometimes God seems to grab my arm and whisper, "You're going in the wrong direction."

God, help me see the bad things in life not as evil forces
working against me but as your loving benevolent hand on my
shoulder, turning me and pointing me in the right direction.
When that happens, I like to think that you smile and say, "He's
only a child and he's still learning."

It's easy to excuse our children for being thoughtless or careless.
"They're only children," we say.
I wonder if God sighs and says about us:
"They're only children."

Those Minor Problems

"I wish she'd get over it," Sam said to me. He referred to Vicki, his wife, of whom he added, "She majors in the minors. Small problems throw her into depression for two or three days. She's having another of her bad times right now."

The latest incident and the one to which Sam referred had happened at the end of the school day on Tuesday. Vicki taught sixth grade, and a parent had come to her after she dismissed her class. According to Sam's report, the parent criticized her teaching methods and said she felt Vicki didn't give her child enough attention.

"Minor stuff," Sam said, "but my wife reacted as if she faced the greatest threat to her career. Teachers get those flaky, demanding parents all the time. She needs to learn to let it go."

I listened to Sam as he told other examples of his wife's major issues. Then he said something that gave me a moment of insight. "I could give her something big to worry about," he said. "Our company has merged with another. We've been told that they will cut 14 percent of the staff in the restructuring. I could be one of those people whose job they eliminate. In fact, yesterday my manager said he had to eliminate two positions in our division and he hinted that I might be one of them. Now *that* is a major concern!"

He was worried, and it was the first I had realized how troubled he was. I talked to him about his worries over the future of his job.

"You do have a major issue and I can understand why you're worried—"

"It's the best job I've ever had and I think I'm good at it." For another minute or two he tried to convince me that he ought to be able to retain his job.

About 20 minutes later Sam got up to leave. "I feel better. Nothing has changed, but I feel better. Now if only Vicki could—"

I quickly said, "I had a thought while we talked, and I'd like to share it with you."

Sam shrugged and showed me he was willing to listen.

"You have a major problem, and I understand. You're worried and deserve to be concerned. After all, it's a big, big problem." He nodded, so I added, "But for me, nothing will change in my life over what happens to you, right? I care, but it's not a major issue for me."

Sam nodded a second time.

"It's a minor issue to me, but to you, it's major—"

"Anyone faced with my situation would feel the way I do," Sam said.

"Really? Maybe one of your co-workers will be relieved. Maybe one of them will laugh and call it a stupid job anyway."

Sam agreed and mentioned a co-worker with that attitude.

"Now think about Vicki. To you, she faces only minor problems in her teaching; but to her, it may be major. The difference is that the difficult, critical parent is her problem and it's not yours; your job is major to you, but minor to me because it's not my problem."

I'm not sure Sam learned much from what I said, but it was a simple but insightful moment for me. I consider it one of the *big* lessons I learned as a pastor.

> *To me a problem may be minor,*
> *but to the person with the problem,*
> *it may be major.*

Furthering My Plans

I had been a Christian for less than a year when I met (and later married) Shirley. I often refer to her as a cradle Christian because she can't remember when she didn't love Jesus Christ. I knew almost nothing about the Christian faith and she was one of my first teachers.

On our second date, Shirley casually mentioned that she spent at least half an hour every day in prayer and another half hour in Bible reading.

"Every day?" I asked, slightly surprised.

"Without prayer and Bible study, my day doesn't go well," she said.

That was enough for me because I wanted to be as good a Christian as she was. The next day I began to develop the daily habit of time alone with God. Because of her example and her encouragement, I've stayed with the self-discipline (most of the time anyway). Over the years I've learned many lessons about prayer; many came slowly, a few involved major spiritual battles and issues, and others are issues over which I still struggle.

I want to tell you about one of them.

It concerns praying for the will of God in my life. I could also call it praying for guidance, seeking direction or simply asking the Lord to "show me the way."

Along with that, from my early Christian days I've believed in opening my heart to God and talking about the things that concern me. That fits most of us.

One of the issues for me has been that I'm sometimes positive that I know what I want, where I want my life or career to go, and I tell God.

I have a friend who quotes a saying from an unknown source: "If you want God to laugh, tell him your plans." I've also laughed at that statement, but it's a little closer to me than I'd like to admit.

My problem is that I tend to tell God how to arrange my affairs. I ask God for success, and that part feels right to me. Where I tend to mess up is that I go on from there and try to figure out ways to achieve the results I want. I'm not condemning myself for that. I'm one of those individuals who agrees that "God helps those who help themselves," even though that statement doesn't appear in the Bible. I'm an active person and I'm ready to do whatever it takes.

But sometimes I get it wrong. Too easily I forget who controls the world. I forget that God is totally in charge of my life. Too frequently my prayers center on asking for divine help to further my plans and desires. I realize we need sensitivity here because God can and does show us how to function or points us in the right direction.

When I become aware, I apologize and remind myself that I'm the servant. That's not quite right: I'm a love slave. That refers to the Old Testament where a slave, when set free, wanted to stay with his master after finishing a period of servitude. The master bored a hole in the servant's earlobe and that classified him as a love slave.

Despite that, I still try to act like the master instead of giving the Great Master the opportunity to direct me and show me what he wants. I can refer to my zeal to serve God. I might even think I've heard God's voice when it's my anxiety or urgency that pushed me on.

Instead I want to try it this way: When I pray, I want to listen and wait for God to speak to me. Unless I'm totally sure that the

Spirit is leading me, I'm learning to hold back and be clear that I've heard the right voice. Too often, I discover that I've fooled myself into thinking God is leading when I really am trying to lead him.

God makes a wonderful guide, but he can't function as a follower or a servant.

God, forgive me for trying to make you
into someone who helps me further my plans.
Teach me instead to rely on you so that
I can further your plans.

Looking at the Unlikely

I don't think I'll ever forget Orlo, even though I can't remember his last name. We were members of the same church for perhaps two years before he left for Bible college.

Orlo came back to our home church after completing his first year and preached at a midweek service. He wasn't very good; more accurately, he was dreadful. Beyond his nervousness, he fumbled his words, repeated sections and rambled. He preached his 53-minute message, which he could easily have delivered within 15 minutes.

As he spoke, I honestly wondered why he wanted to be a preacher. I wasn't trying to be judgmental but I silently prayed that God would show Orlo what he ought to do that didn't involve standing behind the pulpit.

Orlo was the first person I recall meeting that seemed like such an unlikely candidate for a preaching ministry. Since then, I've met many unlikely future leaders—and this applies to business or anything else. Another was Glenn. He was one of the first students I met when I entered seminary. Within minutes after we introduced ourselves, Glenn told me about his facility with Greek (which he had in college) and said, "I'm very good at languages." I felt intimidated by his words.

Before we finished our second year, however, the academic dean asked Glenn to leave the seminary. He couldn't keep up with the work. He had done poorly in Greek, but he did stumble along. When we studied Hebrew during our second year, Glenn seemed totally lost.

Why did God call Glenn? Or had Glenn's zeal been so strong that his desire had overridden the divine voice? I don't know, but I've encountered a number of unlikely people trying to move into positions for which they seem to have no facility.

Or I can talk about writing. I used to do what I called mentoring clinics where I worked with serious writers for three days. Stan came to one, and he knew almost nothing about writing; but to his credit he listened to everything I told him, and at the end he had improved—slightly.

Stan came to a second clinic and made a little more progress, but I didn't have much hope for him. I didn't tell him that.

The reason I didn't tell him was because of Orlo. I've already told you my impression of him (and others said the same thing). Orlo finally graduated from the Bible college in Texas and became pastor of a small church in Oklahoma. Three years later, he visited his parents in our area and our pastor allowed Orlo to preach.

To my amazement, I realized he wasn't the same as he had been years earlier. Something had happened. He had learned poise; his delivery was smooth. He stayed on the topic with two major points, brought the message to an excellent conclusion and finished in 24 minutes. (I habitually time sermons.)

I didn't understand the miracle that had taken place, but I did consider it some kind of unexpected phenomenon. I've since witnessed an amazing transformation with a few others who worked hard and became good students or excellent professionals. I hoped the would-be writer, Stan, could become one of them.

And he has. It took Stan at least three years to master the techniques and principles I had expected him to grasp within weeks, but he stayed at his task. He has now published three books and has kindly acknowledged my help. In two of them he credited me for believing in him.

The truth is, I didn't believe in him. I couldn't see what God saw in choosing an unlikely candidate for service, but isn't that what makes his success even more wonderful?

Have you ever noticed that God chooses
unlikely candidates for service?
I'm one of them.
Maybe you are too.

During the Bad Times

When I've talked to individuals after they've suffered severe loss, I often hear them ask the why question.

- "Why did God do this?"
- "Why did God allow this?"
- "Why did it happen to us? We've tried to follow the teachings of the Bible."

Sometimes I speak to them when they're still in shock, and for them to ask such questions means they're trying to make sense out of their tragedy. I understand that because it happens to all of us. Whenever the unexpected takes place, we need a little time to sort out what happened and to fit events into our personal, logical world system.

Beyond the shock, however, we begin to grapple with the bad things in our lives: "My wife left me for another man and I had no idea she was unhappy," he said.

"I received an email this morning from my boss saying that I was fired and not to come back to work," she wailed. "He even said he'd have my personal items shipped back to me by FedEx."

"We were driving along, careful to observe speed limits when a man had a seizure, collapsed, his car ran a red light and he hit us head-on. My daughter died at impact."

The stories are endless and they're sad, tragic and difficult to face. I understand some of that pain—at least as much as someone else can empathize with those who grieve.

Some of the stories are from individuals I've heard speak of God's goodness. They praise the Lord for a job promotion, the birth of a child or the purchase of a new house. They recognize God at work in their lives and don't hesitate to say so. Those are the good moments, and they're quick to praise God.

But what happens to those same people when events go the other way? What happens when what might have been joyful experiences turn into deep tragedy?

A friend recently lost his wife to a massive coronary, and she had no warning of heart problems. He asked many of the questions I'd heard before. I didn't try to answer the questions, but I tried to offer him words of comfort and encouragement.

About a month later I saw him at church and asked how he was doing. "Not much better," he said. He seemed to be at about the same place he was when we had talked last.

I cared, and I prayed for him each day. Three months later, he still hadn't seemed to make progress. I decided to talk straight to him. "Oh, I get it. God was with you when things went well." I mentioned a large contract his company had won shortly before the death of his wife. I mentioned several other blessings in his life that he had shared with me.

He nodded and smiled when I spoke about them.

"But now, the Spirit of God has departed from your life, right?"

Shock filled his face and he started to argue with me, but I stopped him. "For about three months you've acted as if God has turned away from you."

"You're right," he said. "I focused so much on the loss of my wife that I forgot all the good things the Lord has done for me." He stared out the window. "Maybe I didn't expect hardship or heartbreak. Maybe I thought I deserved only the good things that happened to me."

I listened as he pondered his situation.

"I suppose I sound a little like the Israelites. I took the good for granted, and when things went bad, I complained. Like them, when life became difficult they forgot that God was still with them."

He said nothing more for a long time and then he stared at me and smiled. I hugged him because he didn't need to hear more words from me. He understood.

Isn't it strange? When I fail, I blame God for not helping me. When I succeed, I take the credit.

> *If we know God is with us during the good times,*
> *why would we think God deserts us in the bad?*
> *Isn't that when God most shows he is with us?*

Before the Miracle

Too often we think that we face a situation and need help. We pray and God comes to our rescue. Of course that's true because God specializes in doing the impossible. It's not simply a matter of we pray and God answers. The Lord is already providing a solution before we're aware of the problem.

Although I'd thought of that fact many times, it became a reality to me when we faced a serious financial situation. Three days before we were scheduled to leave for Kenya, we still needed a thousand dollars. We had agreed to go to Africa with a nondenominational "faith" organization. That meant we had to raise all the money for our transportation as well as raise monthly pledges to support us. We never asked for pledges, but the head of the mission board didn't hold us to that part.

We were ready to leave. We thought we had enough money to pay for our airfare to Africa, and that's when we discovered we still needed a thousand dollars.

Shirley and I had agreed that we would never ask anyone for money, and we wouldn't hint. ("We need $4,000 for a car. Will you pray that God will speak to hearts?") Our attitude was that if God wanted us to go, it was the divine responsibility to provide for our needs. We didn't mind begging God, but we didn't feel it was right for us to beg people.

When we faced the reality that we still lacked a thousand dollars, Shirley and I felt we had only one response: We would pray for the Holy Spirit to speak to the right donors. In those days we could cancel airline tickets without penalty, and we considered that perhaps we had been premature. If God wanted us to wait, we were willing to do that.

That morning we were at the mission headquarters, and our young children went out to play with other children. That gave us a few hours to pray fervently. The longer we prayed, the more assured we became that we were on the divine timetable about departing and that we shouldn't cancel our plane tickets.

On our knees we pleaded with God for about two hours before Shirley touched my hand, stood up and said, "I'm at peace." I felt the same way, so we stopped praying. We had no idea what would happen or how God would provide, but both of us knew it was all right.

I assumed we'd get a phone call or perhaps a special delivery letter. Nothing happened that day.

The next day—two days before our scheduled departure— we walked down to the office of our missionary headquarters. No additional money had come in for us.

I was disappointed, but Shirley seemed confident that everything would work out all right.

The next morning—less than 24 hours before we were to leave—as I studied my Bible, part of my scheduled daily reading was Isaiah 65:24: "I will answer them before they even call to me. While they are still talking about their needs, I will go ahead and answer their prayers!"

I read that verse three or four times, and a deep peace came over me once again. It was one of those times when I simply knew that verse was meant directly for me to encourage me and assure me that God was with me and everything was all right.

An hour later, Shirley and I walked toward the cafeteria and passed the office. The secretary raced out and called to us. "It came! It came!" She had received a check only minutes earlier in the mail. It was for the exact amount the board said we needed.

It was a wonderful answer to our prayers, and after lunch, we spent time on our knees in our room giving thanks to God. But there was something even more important to me than the supply of the money that morning.

The couple who sent the money added a note that read something like this: "We realize that the Murpheys will be leaving soon and we want to send this before they leave. We hope it's not too late." I laughed after the office manager read the note and said, "It's not too late, but just in time."

Before I could tell Shirley the verse I had read that morning, she quoted it to me.

That's when I learned something that would continue to occur repeatedly. God had already sent the answer on its way before we knew we had a need.

Sometimes miracles come from behind the scenes. God is already actively providing the answer before we ask. For me, that's been an amazing concept. It's not only that God answers *after* we pray. God answers *before* we pray.

"Our need didn't catch God unaware," I wrote to our contributors. "He knew what we lacked before the need arose. Your letter was postmarked *two days* before we prayed."

God answers after we ask;
sometimes God answers before we ask.

Needing Appreciation

When I was in college, during our chapel services an extremely talented student named Dan played the organ and sometimes the piano. I don't know much about music, but I had enough musical sense to appreciate the rarity of his talent.

The students and faculty members also recognized his special gift. In a number of chapel services, speakers pointed to him and thanked Dan for his playing.

I remember his name only as Dan, but I can still envision his long fingers as they seemed to caress the keys. He was a quiet, non-mixing type, and I didn't know him well.

I was a commuting student who lived almost an hour's drive north of the Chicago suburb where I studied. Dan lived in the college dorm. One day the weather reporters called for a heavy snow. It started shortly after I reached the college and it became so heavy, I decided to stay overnight. (I had brought a change of clothes and toiletry items in case I had to do that.)

The next morning Dan and I were the first ones to show up for breakfast, and we sat together. I told him—as I had several times previously—how much I enjoyed his musical talent.

Dan smiled and focused on his cereal. Something about the way he responded made me wonder if I had said something wrong.

After I asked, he shook his head. "It's not that you said anything wrong; it's that I'm only a musician. God gave me talent and I use it to play for others."

At first I couldn't figure out the problem. Then it hit me. "Everyone sees you as a musician, but you feel no one sees you as a person."

Dan smiled. "That's it. I hadn't been able to put it into words but, yes, that's it exactly. I'm gifted, but I'm more than my gift. No one here at the college knows me—not really. I practice every day for several hours, and I'm not one of those guys who stands out in the crowd, but—"

"But you'd like to be appreciated for who you *are*."

"I wish they would say they appreciate my studiousness or even the way I comb my hair."

After Dan left, I thought about him. Although he was gifted, to many of us Dan the person had became invisible. Perhaps that's an exaggeration, but few of us thought of Dan the student. I certainly hadn't thought of him apart from his music. So I was at fault as much as any of the others.

For the rest of that year, Dan and I talked occasionally. I avoided discussing his music or complimenting him on his playing. I tried to focus on him. One day I asked, "What do you plan to do when you graduate?"

He told me that everyone had assumed he would attempt to go into recording or some kind of professional music venue. "I love to play, but it's not my profession. It's a gift that I want to give others to enable them to worship better."

He confided that he dreamed of living in a Spanish-language country and teaching Bible. That's exactly what he did. The last I heard from Dan, he was living in Peru and teaching Bible and English in a secondary school. He was also the pianist in the local church.

Dan found a way to be more than his gifts. I'm not sure those who are gifted always learn to do that.

I thought of Dan a couple of years ago when I keynoted at a writers conference with perhaps 250 people present. A number of the conferees said to me the next day or so about my writing, "I love the way you write," or "I feel the words on the page when I read your prose."

Naturally I loved hearing all the nice things, but by the end of the conference, I thought about the conversation with Dan many years earlier. Now I understood.

I didn't get the singular line of appreciation the way Dan did, but I received enough to make me understand. We like to have our talents appreciated, but we also want people to like us and value us for who we are.

> *All of us want appreciation for our talent;*
> *we need appreciation for our personhood.*

Only to Understand

Maybe other people aren't like me, but from childhood, it wasn't enough for my mother or father to tell me what to do. I also needed to understand the reason. It wasn't defiance but a need for clarity.

"If I understand what you want to achieve, I can do it better," I told my boss when I was in my first job after high school and before I went into the military. I worked that summer for civil service in the time-keeping division. My boss, Louie, liked to give orders, and I didn't object and was ready to do what he asked. Some of his methods seemed antiquated even back then. For example, he wouldn't use a typewriter if he could write a message by hand.

So I constantly asked questions. After he explained what he wanted, my inevitable question (although not always phrased this way) was, "Why do you do it like that?"

"Because it works," he said the first time.

That wasn't good enough for me, so he patiently explained his rationale. (I didn't always agree, but he helped me understand. Because Louie understood that I wasn't being belligerent, we had a good working relationship.)

Sometimes, of course, the desired effect seemed obvious; but if not, I didn't mind asking. Most of the time, people didn't mind telling me. Only once did I have trouble with that question, and that's when I was in the Navy. Our chief petty officer liked to give orders, and he was responsible for 34 of us in the personnel office. When he asked for questions, I usually said I didn't understand the reason or the purpose. He wasn't used to anyone asking, but sometimes he told me. Not always.

One time we had to fill out forms to transfer sailors from training schools to ships or naval bases. One form was essentially a duplicate, although they asked for the information differently. When I brought up the matter and showed him, he nodded but said, "Just do it."

"But it doesn't make sense."

"Just do it." And he paraphrased the old line from Tennyson, "Yours not to reason why, yours but to do or die."

I did what he asked, but it seemed like a waste of time.

I mention that because in my relationship with God, understanding has been a serious concern for me. When I sense God wants me to do something, my attitude has been, "Help me understand and I'll obey."

Yes, that's presumptuous of me, but that's how I used to pray. It wasn't that I hesitated to obey, but I wanted to grasp the reason or the purpose. And when I didn't get explanations I felt unsure and confused. As I write this, I suppose it also shows a sense of arrogance in pushing for explanations. In my earlier Christian days, my petitions came across as demands, and they probably were. It was as if I said, "You owe me an explanation. Give me an explanation and I'll do it."

I hadn't accepted the reality that my heavenly Father doesn't have to explain anything to me. God is sovereign and has a right to do with me as he pleases. He may not explain a thousand things that puzzle me in his dealings with me.

As I've pondered that issue, I've had to face something in my life. It's fear. Not abject fear but more of a feeling that God would let me down. I don't worry that God might ever do such a thing, but deep, deep within has lingered the fear that I might be disappointed. I've accepted the truth that much of my residual fear is transference from my earthly father to my heavenly

Father. Even though I'm aware, the questions and doubts remained for years.

I can only say that I'm still learning. I'm learning to say, "I'll obey, and *if it pleases you*, help me understand." If I don't comprehend, I'll obey anyway. My desire is that one day the question won't even occur to me.

My loving, heavenly Father wants my total obedience and wants me to give it without hesitation. Sometimes I have to remind myself that God asks me only to obey. "'I know the plans I have for you,' says the LORD. 'They are plans for good and not for disaster'" (Jer. 29:11).

Obedience is required; understanding is optional.

Three Forbidden Words

Years ago I decided that I wouldn't use three specific words in dealing with others. I also promised myself that I wouldn't listen when someone else used those same words in talking to me.

Here they are: *ought, must* and *should.*

When I was a child, teachers used those prohibited words, and I was all right with that. But when I became an adult, I made adjustments in my life. By my early thirties, I struck those words from my vocabulary.

When someone used one of the words, I laughingly replied, "Only God and my mother can tell me what I ought to do."

It's not merely a sensitivity to words or not wanting to hear three negative words. It's what lies behind the forbidden threesome.

First, when someone tells me what I must do, it's a subtle but significant tone that says, "I know better than you do. Listen to me and you'll get it right." That other person may be correct. Perhaps not.

The statement probably says more about the other person than it does about me, but I don't feel I'm obligated to heed anyone but the Great Shepherd. He said, "My sheep listen to my voice; I know them, and they follow me" (John 10:27). That's the only voice I'm required to follow.

When God lays one of the demand-words on me, I have no trouble; but who else is qualified to say what's best for me or that the other person knows better than I do? That person may, but what if he or she doesn't?

Second, it implies that I'm not bright enough to figure it out on my own and I must allow someone else to explain or show me what I need. It's close to the first reason but this puts the emphasis on my inability to know what's best for me.

Third, it comes across as if to say, "If you want to live a blessed life, here is the absolutely final word and immutable law." No one actually says those words, but it comes across to me like that.

I've also noticed that most people who say the forbidden words expect compliance from their listeners. They seem certain of the right thing to do. Maybe part of my resistance is that I'd like to be that confident about the right action or the correct decision.

By contrast, we read the three words all through the Bible, and it's important to point out the distinction. Because I am a child of God and will always be subservient to the divine Master, my role is to listen and nod in agreement (even if I don't like what I read or what I sense the Spirit says to me).

When God uses those words, not only do they come from the Sovereign who created me and who sustains my life, but they also come to me out of love. I truly believe God wants me to live a wonderful, fulfilled life. I don't need to question the Spirit's wisdom.

When I hear the divine whisper (and God doesn't seem to shout), "You should . . ." followed by a course of action, it's a gentle voice that has a singular purpose for my life. "And we know that God causes everything to work together for the good of those who love God and are called according to his purpose for them. For God . . . chose them to become like his Son" (Rom. 8:28-29). If we grasp the underlying purpose of all things that transpire, we readily obey the infallible voice. That also gives us choices whether to heed others' fallible advice.

Because of the pure and wonderful purpose God has in my life, I welcome and yearn to hear those three words.

But only from God.

Only from the One who truly knows the right path for me.

I lovingly grant the Holy Spirit permission to
use "ought," "should" and "must" in my life;
to everyone else, they are forbidden words.

33

A True Friend

David Morgan has been my best and truest friend for 30 years. I have a deep relationship with him that continues to grow over the years. We've both worked to strengthen the bond between us. As a result, we've had exactly one argument in all those years, but it wasn't serious enough to cause damage to our friendship. In fact, I think it reinforced our mutual commitment.

I value our connection, and it has become the model for the friendships I want with others. To have that kind of relationship, I had to ask myself several times why David and I have continued for so many years while other connections have faltered or died. I've often said (and mean it) there is nothing I can't talk to him about, and I think the same is true with him. He has been my model for human friendship.

Because we bonded, it has enabled me to define what I want in a true friend. First, I had to decide what I didn't want. I didn't want someone who always told me nice things about myself. That's not a friend; that's a lackey or a sycophant.

I didn't want someone who constantly told me my weakness and wanted to function as my conscience. That's not a friend, but a dictator. Those people intrude on the work of the Holy Spirit in my life. I wanted rebuke when I needed it and then for the other person to leave me alone to process the rebuff. My allegiance is to God, and sometimes I need divine wisdom to think through what I've heard.

True friends don't pester me with, "I'm telling you this for your own good." The people who say those words usually mean they want to rebuke me without taking responsibility for what they say. I once worked with a missionary woman who used that beginning statement of speaking up for my own good. Occasionally she varied it with, "I thought you'd like to know . . ." As soon as she started I knew I had to endure a lecture and directions that started with, "You should . . ." I remember a woman named Eva, who seemed to know everyone's shortcomings and worked hard to show them. But, of course, Eva never had shortcomings.

I would not have called her a true friend, because true friends don't feel they know how I should live my life, and they remain mindful of their own weaknesses and failures.

Twenty years ago I defined a friend in three statements. First, a friend knows my faults. My true friends don't close their eyes to my failures or weaknesses, but they accept that's part of who I am. They accept my imperfections and shortcomings. I don't need to confess to them any of my weaknesses, because they're already aware of them.

Second, they still love me. No matter how weak I am in some areas and how pompous and obnoxious I may be in others, they still care deeply about me. They're the people I can count on when I face pain and hardship.

Third, they have no plan for my self-improvement. That's the real test of friendship. If they truly are my friends, they will pray for me and will ask God to help me, but they'll leave it up to God to help me work it out. They don't try to fix me or change me.

Jesus is the one friend from whom I withdraw that final statement. Obviously, he sees with perfect insight and knows. By contrast, my human friends are like me: Sometimes they know, sometimes they only think they know, and sometimes they're totally wrong.

A true friend knows my faults, still loves me
and has no plans for my self-improvement.

34

Teachers Teach

Shortly before Shirley and I left for Africa, we talked to a woman who had lived in Kenya for nearly four years. She and her husband had been unhappy because they had gone to a remote area with no modern conveniences and almost no contact with other missionaries. "I wanted to talk to someone—anyone—about recipes and what colors to wear. I couldn't stand being isolated and away from people [and by that she meant Caucasians]."

One of the last things she said to me was, "Just remember, the Africans are like children. You need to treat them that way. If you do, they'll respect you and obey you."

I don't remember what I replied, but I could hardly believe what she said to me. If they were like children, whose fault was that? During that couple's days in Kenya, the country was still a British colony and the Mau Mau threatened white settlers. The all-white government invoked strong measures to put down any form of rebellion, and in less than two years, they defeated the uprising.

We sometimes said of those missionaries that they were people of their time and culture. That is, even though believers, they also lived by most of the mores of the people around them.

I didn't like what the former missionaries told me, but an argument with the unhappy couple would have done no good. However, I determined that I would not treat the nationals or anyone as if they were retarded and less than equal.

To my surprise, I had opposition from missionaries, although certainly not all of them. Most of us then-younger missionaries were branded by one of the older ones as "young Turks" because we believed in equality.

I went to Kenya to become a teacher, and my role was to teach African leaders to do evangelism. Within weeks, I decided they could do that better than I could. I taught them a few things and they went out and put the lessons into practice. They were marvelous and did a superb job.

I had gone as their teacher and I taught them. I also found new ways to work with them. I brought national pastors in for seminars and taught them Bible and theology. I started a correspondence course and used whatever opportunities I could to teach.

We foreigners were the teachers; they were the students. That was the understanding of most missionaries. But that wasn't totally true in my experience. Although I went to teach, sometimes I felt I learned more than they did. That may not be accurate, but they taught me many wonderful lessons. And many of those lessons came about because of the way they lived and expressed their faith.

They may have lived in a more primitive society, but one of the most important things I learned from them was to live happily with fewer possessions. The less they had, the more thankful they became. One famine season seemed almost as bad as the biblical famine in the time of Joseph, but it lasted only two years. Instead of hoarding, as many of us would do, they shared with each other what little they had.

They rarely spoke about private possessions, but it was always "our coat" or "our bicycle."

A British missionary friend spoke at a church and, according to African custom, no visitors left without food. As he prepared to leave, the pastor said, "We have nothing to cook for you." He handed the missionary one egg. "This is the best we can do."

Tears filled my eyes when I heard that story. They had so little but were willing to give so much.

I also learned the importance of family and extended family. They accepted me openly and readily. They invited me into their homes. They honored me by giving me an African name. They did that to all foreigners, usually only among themselves, but they used my African name openly, sometimes to the consternation of other missionaries.

But most of all, they taught me about friendship and love. It wasn't a foreign topic to me, because I saw it in their faces and felt it with their words.

One time several women told my wife how much she meant to them, and they were sad that we were leaving the country. Shirley pointed out that another woman was coming—someone who had been there before and who knew the language better than she did.

"She taught us many things, it is true," one woman said, "but you have loved us."

Maybe Shirley and I did teach important lessons, but we were also the learners. Our lives have been far richer for having lived among them.

We can always teach others and share
the knowledge and understanding we've learned.
We can also learn from those we teach.

35

Our True Gifts

I'm a giver and I like to give. It's not anything I have to push myself to do, because it's natural. In Romans 12, Paul refers to a number of spiritual gifts and he writes, "if [the gift] is giving, give generously" (v. 8).

I understand that and I enjoy sharing with others. I remember vividly more than 30 years ago I read, "Whoever is kind to the poor lends to the Lord, and will be repaid in full" (Prov. 19:17, *NRSV*). That verse made a strong impression on me and encouraged me to give even more freely.

Probably this sounds like bragging, but I point out my generous nature to lead to the dark side of my personality. It's true that I gave easily and freely, but I also kept score.

Not that it happened intentionally, yet I remained quite aware of what I did for others. If I gave someone something, especially money, I expected repayment of some kind. I never said that, naturally, but when others did nothing to reciprocate, I felt hurt and unappreciated.

If I helped a troubled family, I didn't expect them to repay the money but I expected appreciation. When I did something at church, it didn't occur to me that I wouldn't receive praise or recognition.

One time I spent a day waxing and polishing the sanctuary floor of a small church where Shirley and I were members. The pastor saw me, waved at me and hurried on his way. He never thanked me for giving an entire day to that floor. Not then and not later. I was hurt. I'm ashamed for my attitude but that's how I functioned in those days.

The realization that prompted change isn't important; it is important that I eventually faced what I had done. It took me years to acknowledge that the best gifts come with no strings attached. In fact, only true gifts have no demands with them.

For several months after my "awakening," whenever I did something for someone, I wanted to assure myself that I did it with no expectation of reciprocation. For several months, I said, "This is a gift. You owe me nothing."

Many of those I helped did nothing for me in return. As strange as that sounds, I'm glad they didn't. God had healed me of my need to get something in return. I was able to say, and to mean, I had given the gift to God, and the individual was the recipient. Whenever someone did reciprocate, it came as a delightful surprise.

Before my spiritual victory, not only did I expect other people to repay my kindness, but I also expected God to repay me. That wasn't grace, but I hadn't gotten that far in my spiritual development.

Quid pro quo is a Latin term that means "something for something" and is a way of saying, "I give you this and I want something of equal value in return." I did that to God as well as to people. I'm ashamed to write those words but I assume there are other generous givers who secretly keep score. If I can face it, I hope they can as well.

To give without expectation has become a powerful part of my life in recent years. It's not what I give or how, but that I give joyfully and know I may never receive anything in return. I'm aware that God sees everything, and what we do for others in secret, God rewards openly. But that's no longer important.

When I helped others, I used to attach strings. I still do, but now they're heartstrings and they don't even require acknowledgment.

It's important, and I'm excited that God gave me the gift of giving to others. I sometimes quote Jubilations 4:4 as my testimony about giving: "Yea and God shoveleth it in and I shovel it out; and behold, the Lord hath the larger shovel."

Here's something else I like to say: I don't work hard for God in order to receive; I work hard because I have received so much.

The best gifts come with no strings attached.
In fact, only true gifts have no strings attached.

On Giving and Receiving

I liked having lunch with Tom. We were both pastors and he seemed to like my company as much as I enjoyed his. Only one thing bothered me: As soon as a waiter laid the check on the table, Tom snatched it. No matter how often I objected or how vocally I protested, he insisted on paying. One time he actually slapped my hand when I reached for the check.

Paying for both our meals was a nice gesture on Tom's part, but I felt we ought to split the cost or take turns buying. No matter how often I protested he remained adamant. "I like doing this," was all he ever said.

Because of his attitude, I felt demeaned, as if I owed him something or that I was deficient in some way. To his credit, Tom never said such a thing and I'm not sure that was his intention.

I write that because giving and receiving has remained a difficult issue for me, and for many of us. We can easily become the benevolent dictator with our generosity. We can make others feel beholden to us, regardless of our attitude in giving.

I can play the Tom-role easily, and I like doing that; however, I haven't been good at receiving, whether it's money, physical help or a compliment. When I'm on the receiving end, it brings up emotional issues with me:

- I'm undeserving.
- I don't want to owe someone.

- I don't like feeling powerless.
- I feel as if the other person must take care of me.

After our house burned, I learned some lessons about receiving. The fire left us absolutely nothing, and neighbors, friends, relatives and strangers rushed to help us. Their kindness touched me deeply. I tried to thank everyone personally and followed up with a letter, but it never became comfortable. My response felt inadequate for their generosity.

My friend Dan Miller gave me a different perspective when we discussed the issue.

"When I give to someone," Dan said, "it makes me feel good." He reminded me of a church member named Russ Hoyle. Before Russ died of cancer, he asked the men's group for help. "All of us who helped felt honored," Dan said. "We felt we had been let inside and felt close to Russ in the act of doing something for him."

That concept hadn't occurred to me. When we receive help, we let others inside. We show our humanity, our weakness and our neediness. Maybe that's part of God's plan for all of us. Maybe we need to let others see the inner parts of our lives.

As I ponder that thought I consider what Paul says in Acts 20:35: "And I have been a constant example of how you can help those in need by working hard. You should remember the words of the Lord Jesus: 'It is more blessed to give than to receive.'"

A now-dead friend used to joke and refer to Acts 20:35 when someone did something nice for him, saying, "You're selfish. You want the greater blessing."

Maybe part of being a receiver is to allow the other the greater blessing. Possibly part of this is to humble us and remind us that all of us need others. Maybe some of us are afraid to let others see how human and needy we are. Perhaps it helps if we remind ourselves that we give for others as an act of love and want them to appreciate our gifts. It's also a good idea to let them express their love and thank them.

When I give *of* myself, I also give *to* myself. Part of the giving is the inner reward of enriching others and being enriched by the experience. True love gives freely. We all know that. True love also receives freely. Some of us struggle with that part of the lesson.

> *I give to others because it's good to do;*
> *I receive from others because it's right to do that.*
> *Both are acts of love.*

Looking at My Face

I was 22 years old and newly married. Shirley and I talked to a man in the church who was in his late seventies. He went out of his way every Sunday to welcome us and call us by name.

"You really like him, don't you?" I asked Shirley as we sat across the aisle from him. The answer was obvious and it was more an observation than a question.

"You want to know the reason I like him so much?" And of course I said yes. "It's his laugh wrinkles."

I'd never heard the term before, but I turned and stared at him. The wrinkles in the corners of his eyes showed his age, but she was right—it was more than age creases. Those marks made his face look as if he were preparing to smile. They also suggested that he had smiled so much in his younger years that his face permanently displayed the joy.

Until Shirley mentioned the man, I hadn't noticed. Since then, however, I've met many people with smile wrinkles. It's often one of the first things I observe when I meet someone like that.

Over the years I've also realized that the face says more about people than we assume. Long before they speak, we already know something about them.

For instance, when I went to my 30-year high school reunion, I saw one of my former classmates. Billy and I had never been friends, but we lived three blocks from each other.

As I stared at him, I kept thinking, *He's lived a hard life.* I hadn't heard anything about him since high school and didn't know what he had done with his life. But it was obvious he wasn't a happy man and that life hadn't been good for him.

A few years later, George, another classmate, mentioned that Billy had died. When I asked about the cause, he said, "He drank himself to death." As he spoke those words, I understood. His face had declared who he was and I could read the results.

Since then I've thought about my own face. I look like this because it's the face I've earned from the years I've lived on this earth. Each day my face declares to the world around me who I am before I say a word.

I mused on that thought a few Sundays ago in church. The woman who sat three rows in front of me had built-in smile wrinkles. As the pastor spoke, she smiled and nodded. It was as if she heard every word he spoke and accepted it as important. That's also the kind of face I see when she's not sitting in church.

The writer of Proverbs said it well: "A glad heart makes a happy face; a broken heart crushes the spirit" (Prov. 15:13). And we've all been around those with turned-down lips and perpetual frowns. Those are the people we tend to move away from quickly.

Here's what I want to point out: Our faces witness to others of our relationship to God. We don't have to force ourselves to become people of the goofy grin or constantly monitor our countenance. But if God is significant in our lives, our faces display the evidence—especially when we're unaware.

I thought of an incident when our oldest child, Wandalyn, was less than three years old. She sat between her mother and me. The pastor preached about God's love and how important it was for us to love others.

"Why is he so mad?" our daughter whispered.

Just then I grasped what she saw. He pounded the pulpit and a frown covered his face. He spoke about love but his face exhibited anger—perhaps anger because we weren't loving. Or perhaps anger because he was giving us the wrong signal about love and it took a three-year-old child to get it.

I don't want to judge the face of another person—and may God help me not to do that. But sometimes those laugh wrinkles are so forceful I'm caught up in the warmth of the smile or the open-faced grin. That's the kind of face I'd like to have.

As I grow in my commitment and knowledge of God, maybe God will give me a joyful countenance. Or at least one that radiates peace. Most of all, I'd like a face that causes others to think about Jesus.

As we get older, our temptation is to look backward and think of the good old days or what life might have been like. What if we reminded ourselves, "This is who I've worked to become"?

I want to live in such a way that when I reach an advanced age, my face will show my attitude and lifestyle without my having to say a word.

I look like this because it's the face I've earned
from the days I've lived on this earth.
Each day my face declares who I am before I say a word.

Hearing It Again

Two years ago, Ralph contacted me because he had started a book about which he was passionate. He talked to me about writing the book for him. Ralph had been a top salesman in the film business, had undergone a dramatic conversion and was trying to find his way in the Christian life.

I met him two or three times and knew it wasn't my kind of project, which was all I could tell him, but I liked Ralph and I was willing to help him any way I could. I gave him some advice and he listened politely. One of the things I suggested to him was that he would probably have to self-publish his book, and I listed several reasons for my opinion.

Ralph dropped out of my life for nearly two years. Other than an occasional group email, I didn't hear from him. He resurfaced at the time I first started this book. We met for lunch and talked for a long time.

At lunch Ralph told me that he had finally decided to self-publish. He went through a long explanation, and I replied, "I said that two years ago."

"You did?"

After I nodded, he mentioned two other decisions that had "finally come to me."

"That's part of the advice I gave you two years ago."

Again he asked, "You did?"

As we talked, I didn't feel I had to be right, and I certainly wasn't smug because Ralph had figured out something I had mentioned to him two years earlier. For several minutes that afternoon, after we parted, I pondered the situation. I had said those things to Ralph and he seemed to understand.

I realized that the first time I had spoken, Ralph hadn't really "heard" me, and that was all right. I told him things that he hadn't been ready to accept. He was convinced that he had a book (and a film to come out of that) that would become the next international bestseller.

I didn't make fun of his dream; after all, who was I to tell him he was wrong? Because he felt so passionate about his immediate plans, I suggested he follow them. (I knew he would anyway.) It took Ralph two years to come to the conclusion I had told him previously.

I could easily have chided him for being so slow in getting the valuable information I had presented, or I could pull back and say to myself, he wasn't ready. I'm not different from Ralph. I face the same issue, and so do all of us: What we're not prepared to accept or learn goes past us, even though we think we receive the message.

My friend David Morgan has pointed out things about me and, at the time, I nod, agree and thank him. But somehow those truths don't always sink into my heart and end up changing my attitude or actions. Sometimes I have to hear the message a second time. Or a third. Maybe more than that.

I thought of my spiritual life and felt slightly ashamed. I've lost track of the number of times I've read completely through the Bible. At one time, both Shirley and I read it at least once a year; a few times I did it every six months. It's not that the Bible is a strange book to me. Like many people familiar with God's sacred words, I hear a verse and I can often cite the reference or at least the context.

And yet I don't really know the Bible. I've read verses 20 times and moved on. On the twenty-first time, I've "heard" the verse differently. I grasped the message.

Why? The answer seems obvious. Like Ralph, I didn't comprehend the true message until I was ready.

I've sometimes prayed this way: The first time I hear what
I need I may act on it. Yet I hesitate because sometimes those insights may be preparation for the time when I'll be ready to
make changes.

> *No matter how many times I hear something,*
> *I will deny what I'm not prepared to accept.*

Things of Value

This morning I thought about a college classmate friend named James. He had all the attributes of a male model—tall, slender, handsome, with black hair and green eyes. More than his looks, James was also one of the brightest individuals I met during my college days.

We didn't have many classes together, but he was always the star no matter what subject he studied. He had the kind of mind that absorbed information immediately and was insightful enough to know how to interpret and feed it back through his own frame of reference.

I wasn't like James. In some ways I'm quick, but I worked hard in school. I received good grades but I could say I earned them by my hard work. One classmate used to tease me, "If I worked as hard as you do, I'd have good grades too." Of course he didn't work hard, so how would anyone know?

Even though classes weren't always easy for me, I admired James. I didn't resent him for being bright and insightful. Instead I wished I were more like him. Perhaps this sounds exaggerated, but it's true, and I was one of his admirers. That's why we became friends. Early in our relationship I said, "I like people who are as bright or brighter than I am. That's why I want your friendship."

We didn't go to anything outside of college classes but we often spent our breaks together before chapel services at 10:00. A few times we became so absorbed in opening up to each other, we skipped chapel.

On the day of our graduation, I said to James, "I can see a fantastic future for you. You could probably succeed at almost anything you chose to do."

I haven't seen James since college. I knew his aunt slightly and she wrote me a few letters (in the days before email) while we were in Africa. When I answered, each time I asked how James was doing.

She didn't go into detail and usually said, "James is fine." Or "James married a lovely young woman named Helen."

James's aunt died, and after that I lost all contact with him. From time to time I'd meet other former classmates, and I usually asked about James. I wanted to get in touch with him and renew our friendship. No one seemed to know how to reach him.

So far as I know—and it's been years since I've heard about him from anyone—James didn't use those wonderful talents. He married, divorced and remarried twice. He never held any position below a low-management level.

For a long time I wondered why and how James had squandered that great ability. One day I had an inkling to the situation: Everything came easy to James.

His good looks opened many doors and his mental agility kept them open. The problem, however, was that because everything came easy it required no effort on his part. I rethought our classroom days when James rarely studied and sometimes smiled indulgently at me when I groaned about the hours I put into my class work.

Maybe that's how life is for all of us. The natural or easy things often seem insignificant. If we work hard for something, it becomes valuable because of the effort and time we've invested.

Isn't it the same principle in our spiritual lives? In our marriages? In everything we do? If we grasp that something is important, we invest ourselves in that activity. God's gifts are free but they're not like ripe fruit hanging on the lowest limbs of the tree, waiting to be plucked. The best fruit often seems above our heads and we have to work to reach it.

We don't have to be Christians long before we know that God asks us to be disciples—that is, learners. Some may have more spiritual aptitude than others, but God gives to those who seek him and obey.

That's of comfort to me. James was brighter and more talented, but from what I've heard, he put no serious effort into working hard.

One of the best compliments I ever received came from Bob, who was also a classmate. We didn't see each other for more than 30 years after graduation. "What I remember most about you," he said, "was your commitment. I knew nothing would ever stop you from following the Lord."

Tears filled my eyes because I had no idea that anyone else saw that about me. I know that, even in college, I yearned to be the best Christian and the most faithful disciple I could become. For me, it seemed as if I had farther to travel than most of my classmates. Maybe.

Or maybe I put in the effort because growing in my relationship to Jesus Christ became the focus of my life.

Nothing of real value comes easily or quickly.
Part of the value lies in the difficulty to reach it.

The Why Question

Eddie and I had known each other since third grade and we stayed in touch through the years. Ten years ago, I visited my hometown and had lunch with him and we caught up with life. It took us perhaps half an hour to finish with do-you-remember-when stories.

As we finished our meal, I thought we were ready to leave but Eddie leaned forward and stared directly at me and said, "I hate my life!"

His fierce statement shocked me, and I listened to the litany of unhappy events since his early days in the work force. It was one sad tale after another. "Is that all there is in life?" he asked. Before I had a chance to answer, he shook his head. "Why? Why is my life so miserable?"

I didn't have an answer and I don't think he wanted one; I think Eddie only wanted to confide in me and for me to listen.

That happened ten years ago. I saw Eddie recently; he still hates his life and he still asks why. I thought of Eddie this morning shortly after I awakened. I focused on him because I pondered the why question—one I've pondered many times in recent years. Why? Why? A number of things had happened in my life during the past two weeks, and I felt overwhelmed. *Why is all this happening to me? Why is it happening now?*

I don't understand it and I can't figure it out, but here is my big question: Why is God so good to me? Why has the Lord given me so many great blessings? Why do I feel so loved? Why do I feel special? Why has God chosen me to write and to teach? What did I do to deserve this wonderful life?

It's a mystery to me and I don't suppose I'll ever solve it, but it doesn't stop me from asking the why question. In times like this I find myself quoting the beautiful benediction from Ephesians 3:20: "Now all glory to God, who is able, through his mighty power at work with us, to accomplish infinitely more than we might ask or think."

That verse becomes powerful to me because it reminds me that God is far, far more generous than I could ever imagine. I have so much more in material possessions and healthy relationships than I ever expected. But why me?

I think of the story of young Solomon and his coming to the throne. In a dream, God asked him what he wanted, and because Solomon didn't ask selfishly, God granted him far more than he asked.

That's how I feel. I hope the difference between Solomon and me is that I make use of what the Lord provides. I can say that I'm more aware of God's grace and presence in my life than I've ever been. So many times in my life I've been aware that individuals reached out to us. Especially after our fire, hundreds of people affirmed us, cared for us and expressed their sympathy and love.

But I still ask: *Why, God? Why are you so good to me?* Maybe that's why we call it grace.

> *If I figure out a reason for God's love,*
> *I have the wrong answer.*

Your Love Lesson

He's a man I hadn't liked very much, whom I'll call Marc. He bragged about his accomplishments and his words sounded impressive. I wouldn't say he lied, only that he overextended the truth. He sometimes made promises to do things but rarely accomplished them. I could list a few of his weaknesses, but the point is that I felt a bit smug in my attitude toward him. I did things; he only talked about doing them.

When I compared myself to Marc, I felt a trifle superior (all right, vastly superior). I realized my attitude was wrong, and each day I prayed for him. I often said, "God, I know you love Marc, but . . ."

Although I prayed each day for Marc, I usually said those words and presented a list of things I didn't like about him. I prayed that the Holy Spirit would help him to become more honest about his accomplishments and keeping his promises. Sometimes I pointed out that Marc had a bad temper, and more than once I had been the object of his wrath.

Marc was also a deacon at the church where we worshiped, and that bothered me. Marc's position was one more topic that I talked to the Lord about frequently. "Shouldn't someone in that position be a little more honest? More spiritual?"

In retrospect, my prayers were judgmental and unkind. I saw Marc with the worst of motives and the poorest of excuses. But to my credit, and probably the one thing to my credit, I continued to pray for him each morning.

One predawn morning while I was running, I heard myself say, "God, I know you love me as much as you love Marc."

As I listened to my own words, I repeated them. As strange as they sounded, it was truly, honestly, the first time I had connected God's love and Marc together. I paused on that darkened street and sat down on the pavement for several minutes. Sometimes I sit and ponder when I'm overwhelmed with a new revelation.

I had focused on his flaws; I had seen him in the most negative manner. Not once had I focused on him as a loved child of God. Now I saw Marc differently and begged God to forgive me for my proud attitude. The truth came through to me. God's love and blessings aren't about achievements or the lack of them. Divine love for us isn't based on our faithfulness.

As strange as it may sound, when I rephrased my thinking to remind myself that God loved me as much as he loved Marc, deep peace came over me.

As I returned to my run, I kept thinking, *God loves Marc. His achievements aren't my business and neither are his failures. He's responsible to the Lord and not to me. That's part of what makes divine grace so wonderful.*

For many mornings after that, I continued to pray for Marc. I started to talk casually to him and he joined the Sunday School class I taught. Over the next few years I began to understand him better and can say that I truly learned to love the man and felt closer to him. We became friends, and I prayed differently after that—I praised God for my friend Marc.

Thank you, God, that you love me
as much as you love other people.

Remembering Responsibility

Our house burned down in February 2007, and it was a terrible loss to Shirley and me. I hated losing all our possessions. Even now I still miss my son-in-law, who died in the fire. I wish it had never happened. I want to be clear about that.

But it happened. I can't change the sad reality.

Three months after the fire, I gave the opening keynote at the Greater Colorado Christian Writers Conference. I mentioned the fire only because several people asked me if I would say something about it.

After I finished, a woman came up to me, hugged me and thanked me. "Just one question," she said. "What's the most important thing you've learned from that tragedy?"

"That's easy to answer," I said. "I've learned afresh (and on a deeper level) that God is sovereign." We know that and I probably hear it said at least once a month among serious Christians.

However, I have to admit that although I spoke of God's sovereignty it didn't become a powerful, exciting theological and personal concept to me until weeks after our fire.

But it did become a reality in retrospect, and it was more than merely repeating the words, "God is in control," although that's true. It has become far richer and stronger for me.

For example, hours after the fire, a friend came to see me and we stared at the smoking remnant of our house. We must have talked for 20 minutes before I said something—something I hadn't even thought about.

"God has been preparing me for this."

As I spoke those words, I knew they were true. Over the past decade, for example, my experiences pointed me in the direction of divine sovereignty. Things hadn't always worked out as I wanted or planned, but my faith and commitment were strong enough that I kept moving forward even during the bad times.

Eight months after our fire, a special friend and editor called me. He was discouraged and unsure about what to do next. He wasn't happy in his position and he was sure he should leave it. He wasn't worried about money or supporting his family. His concern was the right thing to do.

I said something that I wouldn't have thought of a year earlier: "Isn't God responsible to show you what to do? Your duty is to obey. It's not up to you to make that decision." He seemed delighted at my response.

As I shared those words, I added, "If you're still unsure what you're supposed to do, ask God to show you. It's not your task to figure out your next step. That's God's job. Let God do what he's supposed to do. You may need to wait and the answer may not come immediately, but that's still the divine prerogative."

"You're right," my friend said, "I'm in God's hands." He smiled and said, "But then, that's where I've been all along."

I took my own words to heart. They had come out unplanned, but I knew I was also speaking to myself. I ask and that's natural, but I haven't always waited for God to assert his will. Too often I've acted without God's guidance.

Since the fire, I've gone back to that conversation many times. I believed those words then; I believe them even more today. Because God is sovereign, it means that God is totally in control.

> *God's responsibility is to guide; mine is to obey.*
> *Although I often remember my role,*
> *I sometimes forget God's.*

Beginning Again

When our family returned after nearly six years in Kenya, we owned nothing but our clothes (all badly out of style), a portable typewriter and six crates of books. I enrolled in seminary and we rented an unfurnished apartment. We had to start life again with no possessions. The pastor of a local church loaned us beds. Someone in the student housing complex donated a sofa. People from the church provided a TV, ironing board and a few other household items.

As we acquired each thing, we accepted them as special gifts and valued each item highly. We had nothing, so any gift looked wonderful.

I often thought of what I said to my family before we returned from Kenya. I said, "We get to start over again. We're going to the South (Atlanta) where I've never been before. We'll make new friends and we'll start a new way of life."

It was a new life and it was difficult at times, but it was also exciting. "I have a chance to redefine my life," I wrote to several friends. Seminary helped me to redefine my theology. The new people around me influenced my attitude.

That happened a long time ago. Over the years, we acquired more things, better quality furniture, plenty of clothes, a computer and (of course) more books.

When our house burned down, we lost all of our possessions. "I can begin again," I said to my best friend David. "How many people can do that?"

For the second time it meant starting over with new clothes, furniture, a computer and a car—the obvious things.

Shirley and I did that and without complaining. But beginning again is more than accumulating new possessions. It means a chance to leave behind the old patterns of behavior. It's a chance to look at life and ask, "How do I want to live—starting right now?"

In the process I realized that any of us can start over anytime we choose. But few of us make that decision. To make a new start demands drastic changes. It involves uncertainty about the present as well as the future. *What if . . . ?* questions fill our minds.

There are always obstacles and uncertainties. And not everyone can face that kind of challenge. It's safer and easier not to change and to hold on to our way of life. I wouldn't have started over again if I hadn't been forced to do so. Yet, I'm grateful I've been able to rethink my life.

I'm thankful for the kindness of others. Many people, including strangers, did so much to help us. I looked at each of those gifts as special. I decided I wanted that to be my attitude for the rest of my life. I was forced to begin again, but what if I chose to start over? What if I chose a new place to live or a new profession? New friends? All of that is possible.

For instance, I had a friend named Doug, and we'd been friends for a long time. In those days, Doug had been exactly the kind of friend I needed, and we did exciting, fun things together. But Doug didn't change, or so it seemed to me. Ten years later, he still wanted to do the things we had done a decade earlier, and his ideas and viewpoints on life hadn't expanded. He was still Doug. This isn't to rail against him, because that was his choice. He stayed the same person he had always been; *I had changed.* Because I changed, the relationship couldn't ever be the same again.

I started again to seek new friends. In the early days of my new quest, I quietly eliminated Doug. I faced some guilt, and I wasn't rude, but I slowly drifted out of his life. New friends have come into my life, and they're the ones I can talk to *now* about the exciting things . . .

Yes, each day can be like a new beginning. What would our lives be like if we said, "Today I can choose to redefine my life. Today I can start again"?

God, remind me that today I can choose to redefine my life.
Today I can start again.

Comparing Ourselves

I recently spoke with Philip, a writer I've known slightly for about 15 years. Shortly after we first met, I learned he had written a book that sold well. When I read his book, as well as several of his magazine articles, I decided he was a much better writer than I. "I'll probably never be as good as he is," I said to one of my friends.

Philip moved out of the area and we lost track of each other. He continued to write and averaged a book every two or three years. He made his living as a journalism instructor in a state university.

At a conference, we saw each other for the first time since his move from Atlanta. We had lunch together, and one of the first things he said was, "I wish I could write as well as you do."

"You have to be kidding."

"I assure you that I am not."

I shook my head and said I found it difficult to believe those words. When I told him about my comparison years ago (and also that I was a little jealous), we both laughed.

"I've been secretly jealous of you since I read your first articles," Philip said. He told me some of the things he liked about my writing, and I was shocked. My only comment, which I made several times was, "I had no idea."

I learned something significant from that interchange. When we sincerely compare ourselves to others, we experience negative feelings and sometimes feel inferior, and in my case, jealousy. Other emotions arise such as insecurity and a sense of unworthiness.

We focus on what we're *not* instead of who we are. As long as we feel the need to compare, we can't win. Now, most of us have compared ourselves with others who have failed or been unsuccessful and we have felt smugly superior; but that's not the kind of comparison I mean. This is the kind where someone is good at a task and we recognize the skill or the talent because it's something at which we would like to excel.

In those instances, we see others as those who are more talented, achieve more, get better breaks, more recognition or are better qualified.

A few years after Philip moved away, I decided not to focus on others' achievements, but on my own. I can only be me, and my task is to be the best Cec Murphey I can. Some people are more gifted than I am; some are less able. My responsibility is to be faithful to who I am and what I can do.

What brought me to that place is that one day I read chapter 21 of John's Gospel. I thought of Peter's question to Jesus after the Lord informs Peter how he (Peter) will die. Instead of focusing on himself, Peter points to John and asks, "What about him?"

"What is that to you? You must follow me," Jesus says (John 21:22, *NIV*).

Here's the practical thing I've learned to do: I pray for those of whom I'm tempted to feel jealous. I ask God to bless them as richly as possible. Their success has no bearing on my achievements. Their success doesn't diminish mine. The more I champion others, the less I need to compare and the greater my level of inner peace.

If, instead of focusing on John or Tom or Alice or Edith, we focus on Jesus, we don't get caught up in comparison. We

see ourselves as God's servants and realize how deeply God
loves us.

When we compare ourselves with others,
we feel we're losers;
when we compare ourselves with Jesus,
we know we're loved.

Convenient Compassion

"Any advice?" the man emailed. He had joined the Stephen Ministry in his church. (Stephen Ministry is a voluntary organization that started more than 30 years ago to provide one-on-one Christian care to hurting people.) Because I knew of that ministry, he thought I might be able to guide him.

His question made me think of what I call "convenient compassion." That is, people will volunteer and give of themselves to others—providing it doesn't disrupt their schedule too much. They'll involve themselves for short-term caring and express love and sympathy, and whatever others need—as long as that commitment doesn't interfere with the givers' plans.

I became aware of convenient compassion years ago when Shirley and I were full-time caregivers. Edith was near the end of her life and needed Depend diapers. During that time, Shirley reluctantly left for a women's convention after she had assured herself that Edith knew how to take off old diapers and put on clean ones.

The day after Shirley left, Edith became confused, couldn't figure out how to change her own diaper and made a terrible mess. No matter how much I begged, she was too modest to allow a man to come into her room or let me offer any help. In a state of panic, I started to make phone calls. The county agencies were closed for the weekend.

Out of desperation, I called three nurses in our church. All of them offered advice. When I asked, "Could you come and help me?" I received vague excuses from two. The third changed the subject. I got the message: It wasn't convenient.

Before she became extremely ill, Edith had attended a different church from the one we did. Not knowing what else to do, I called the pastor's wife. "I'll be there within the hour," she said. True to her word, she came and brought Tillie with her. Tillie was the full-time caregiver of a paralyzed husband and had to find someone to stay with him so she could help Edith. The two women spent more than three hours cleaning up Edith and the mess she had made to the bed and the room.

I don't write this to rebuke those three nurses. Their attitude made me look at my own "convenient compassion." I like to help, and I admit that too often I volunteered—but it had to be on my timetable. And it seemed that the most demanding situations occurred when I was already overwhelmed with a heavy load of responsibilities. Why did the cries for help come on those days when I was busiest?

Or would my reaction have been the same no matter when they asked? Probably. My concern was for me, my activities and my lifestyle—in short, my convenience.

I've reflected more fully on my attitude when people need compassion that involves setting aside time. I made a few significant promises to myself. One of them is that I would move beyond convenient compassion. However, I wouldn't let people abuse my time, and there are always a few who want to suck energy out of us. I want to live so that the words of Jesus reflect my lifestyle: "Your love for one another will prove to the world that you are my disciples" (John 13:35).

I'm slowly learning to do the right thing because it is the right thing, even when it's not opportune. In fact, perhaps compassion truly begins when it doesn't fit into our schedules.

As I think of the story of the Good Samaritan, it wasn't convenient for him to help the half-dead man on the Jericho road, but he did (see Luke 10:25-37).

God, help me to do the right thing because it is the right thing,
even when it's not convenient.

My Superior Mode

I sat on the park bench for almost an hour, and most of that time I felt uncertain and a little frustrated because I didn't know what God wanted me to do. Four years earlier I had resigned from the pastorate to write full time. So far I had made a living, but money problems loomed in front of me. A large, unexpected bill caused me to worry about my financial future.

As I sat there, I took out paper and pen and added up all the regular expenses to decide how much money I needed to earn each month to stay ahead of the expenses. After I arrived at the number, my next step was to figure out what I needed to do to bring in that amount of money each month. Without going into detail, I finally decided I needed to do five things each month, and one of them was to write and sell a minimum of two articles to a magazine. If I did all five tasks, I could probably make the bottom line of expenses. Two articles didn't sound like much; however, when I thought that meant writing 24 of them in a year, panic began to sneak into my thinking.

I went back to fretting over expenses and income and felt increasingly confused. Just then I stopped. That's when I received that aha! moment of insight. I was doing it all wrong: I had tried to make decisions from my inferior mode.

I probably knew the terms "superior mode" and "inferior mode" from someplace, but they hadn't gotten into my consciousness. I realized that if I made choices from my superior mode I would be happier and my decisions would be correct. The inferior mode usually led in the wrong direction.

Here's how my superior mode works. I make my best decisions when I trust my instincts. (Call that my guts, feelings or intuition.) Often the decisions involve or produce emotional responses such as deep peace, great joy or the sense that a burden has lifted.

By contrast, when I work from my inferior mode I start down the path of logic and analysis. That's when I get into trouble; I reason things out and my answers appear logical—and they are. The reasoning isn't wrong, but the way of reaching the decision is faulty.

That day in the park, I realized I had allowed a money problem to interrupt my peace of mind. Instead of tackling the issue from my superior mode, I had resorted to my lower form of decision-making. Some of my friends make their best moves by a careful, thoughtful gathering of evidence before they decide. That would be their superior mode, but it's not mine.

As I sat in solitude on the park bench, I turned over the financial problem to my superior mode. I didn't know where the extra money would come from or how I would handle the unexpected expense. Yet as I relaxed, I had a sense that things would work out. That deep sense of peace pushed away the panic and uncertainty. Although I didn't know how, I knew I would be able to pay all my bills when they were due. Less than a week later, a publisher called me with a rush project and sent me an advance before I wrote a word.

The lesson I learned that day in the park has served me well. Whenever I'm in a situation where I have to make a serious decision, and I start slipping into my inferior mode, I know it's likely to be wrong. I'm learning to rely more fully on my intuitive sense, that is, on my superior mode.

When we respond to God to guide through our superior mode, we don't make mistakes; when we listen to our inferior mode, we often fail.

Starting with Problems

We face problems daily. We overcome most of them, stumble over a few and lose an occasional struggle. Many times I think we wish they'd go away and we'd never have to face them.

One time when I talked about a series of tough issues I faced, my friend Sam said, "Problems never leave you where you started."

"I certainly hope so," I said, and we talked about other things. After Sam left, I considered the implications of his statement. Some individuals see hardships as the pressures and evils of life stalking them. "The devil has been after me all week," they say. "Everything went wrong yesterday," another says.

For years I thought of problems as interruptions in my otherwise happy life. I wonder how many times I've prayed for them to go away. During the past few years, however, I've been able to take a different view.

I've heard motivational speakers say, "Don't call them problems; call them opportunities." I've often thought, *It's easy for you to say that to us, but how do you respond when your tough times strike?*

I still wouldn't call them opportunities, because they are quandaries and difficulties. They represent something over which we have to struggle and overcome. We learn from them, but I suspect that when problems hit no one wants to focus on gaining new insights. We want to win over the issue or have it go away.

When our son, John Mark, was young, one of the things I often said to him when he faced challenges was, "Think of this as a learning experience."

One day an exasperated 10-year-old boy put his hands on his hips and said, "Dad, I've already learned too many things."

He meant that he wasn't in the mood for a learning experience. He just wanted to get through the ordeal. I understood, and it had been unkind of me to sound so patronizing. I haven't liked it when people have given me simplistic answers for complicated predicaments.

Instead of ranting or groaning when we encounter those "opportunities" or hardships, what if we accepted the struggles as divinely appointed lessons for our growth? (That's true anyway.) Our responses to those trials shape our lives and have eternal consequences. Because of them, we can become better, stronger and more spiritual people when we encounter setbacks and endure hardships. For years, I've known this truth intellectually, but sometimes it takes awhile for knowledge to catch up with experience. Besides, when we're in the midst of chaos, we don't think about what we'll learn afterward.

These thoughts came about because of something Helena Smrcek once said as she drove me to the Toronto airport. She knows about my childhood and asked how I could be the kind of person I am after having such a traumatic background. "It's called grace," I said.

Afterward, I thought about my past. I realize that I am who I am today because of those problems—and not in spite of them. I've learned to understand others' pain, rejection, discouragement and abuse. I understand because I've experienced similar issues and allowed them to shape my life in a positive way. Because of God's grace I'm a better person for those experiences.

Sam was absolutely right: Problems never leave us where we started. As we struggle with them, we can learn from them and become better equipped to face the next major battle.

Problems never leave us where we started.
As we struggle with them,
we can learn from them and grow.

Changing Others

Whenever I read an article about changing or improving our lives, the author usually inserts a comment that says, "You can't change anyone else. You can only change yourself."

I've said the words myself, but now I disagree. "Sometimes we can change others, but we do it indirectly."

Here's an example of what I mean. Christmas Eve morning I called the office of our medical insurance provider. Three weeks earlier I had gone for a hearing test. The audiologist had barely started the examination when the electricity went out for the entire community. After we waited 20 minutes, we learned that a transformer had blown and that it would take several hours to repair. She made another appointment for me and assured me that I wouldn't be charged twice.

I returned a week later and had the examination. The following week I received a bill for my copayment for the second time. That's when I called the insurance office. After punching various numbers, a cool-voiced woman identified herself as Tammy. I started to explain my problem and she cut me off. "Just give me your insurance number."

I did. She asked other questions for identification but her tone sounded surly. When I had to look for my insurance number she said, "It's right there on the top left of your bill." I told her, "Hold while I check." She clicked off. I must have waited a full minute before she returned to the line.

During that time, I thought about Christmas season and silently thanked God for the quality of my life. In the background, a CD of Christmas carols played softly. I decided not to let her brusque tone bother me.

When she came back on the line she said, "I'll have to do research on this. It will be early January before I get back to you."

"That's all right." I assured her that I understood. "I don't want to push you; I only wanted to report it. Please call whenever it's convenient." She thanked me in a voice only slightly less brusque.

I also said, "You're probably rushed and you don't need another pushy client demanding you put his papers on top of the pile."

"Thank you for calling," she said in a warm voice.

Less than two hours later, Tammy called. "I wanted you to know that I've taken care of the matter."

"So soon? That's wonderful." I told her how much I appreciated her doing that so quickly. She assured me that it was her pleasure, and the tone of her voice made her words believable.

Now I'll go back to the matter of changing others. Her frosty voice could have changed me into an angry, irate policyholder. I could have demanded that she take care of it *now*. I could have railed against the company's inefficiency. Had I behaved like that, she would have changed me. Instead, she changed. Her return phone call made that clear.

So how can we say that we can't change another person? Some might want to equivocate and say, "We can *influence* others." True, but if we influence them, isn't that changing them?

My attitude and words had changed her, but that's not the point. I wasn't interested in changing Tammy; I was committed to enjoy God's blessings. I focused on the joyfulness of the Christmas season and listened to "O Come, All Ye Faithful."

Maybe we *are* most effective in changing others when we focus on changing ourselves.

> *If we focus on being who we are*
> *and refuse to let another's attitude upset us,*
> *we might actually change them.*

"You'll Like Paul"

"You'll like Paul. Everybody does," June said. "He writes well, and he's one of the most hardworking writers I know." Her list of qualities went on, almost like a product-placement commercial.

By the time she finished, I had decided to think of Paul as a friend. After all, I liked June and she liked Paul; I like most people, so I knew I'd like him.

The following week I met Paul. *I didn't like him.*

I wondered how June could have said all those wonderful—although obviously mistaken—things about him. I found it painful to suffer his opinionated remarks. Not only did he have strong views about everything, but he also said them in such a way that made it sound as if anyone who didn't agree must be stupid or ignorant.

In each encounter, Paul became more obnoxious, and for several months, I prayed diligently for him. "Lord, if you'd only give him a little tact. He comes across as the final authority." In spite of my prayers for his improvement, Paul got worse.

One night after the writing group left, Martin lingered. "Are you okay?" he asked. When I didn't answer, he asked, "Do you want to tell me about it?"

"I can tell you in one word: *Paul.*" But I didn't stop with one word. My list of grievances gushed out.

"Do you think Paul does those things on purpose?" Martin asked.

"No, that's the problem. If he did it deliberately, I'd confront him. That's just the way he is."

"Has it occurred to you that Paul believes he's right about what he says?"

"That's also the problem. He's so sure about everything!"

Martin continued to ask questions that forced me to reexamine my attitude. I didn't realize it then, but each probe pushed me to concede a little more of my pent-up animosity.

"Do you think he likes you?" Martin asked.

"Probably not. Why should he?"

"I had lunch with Paul a few days ago. He mentioned how much he had learned from you." Paul had referred to an article I had ripped apart and he told Martin he had known it wasn't good, but he didn't know how to fix it. Because of my suggestions, he revised it and sent it off.

"Paul said *that*?"

Martin took my arm and led me through the hallway. We stopped in front of a full-length mirror. "What do you see?"

"My reflection—"

"You're getting close. Has it occurred to you that when you look at Paul you're looking into a mirror? That you're seeing in him the things you don't like about yourself?"

My immediate response was to reject such a preposterous statement. I opened my mouth to refute his words, but I couldn't speak. It was one of those "gotcha" moments. Martin smiled and allowed silence to control the conversation.

Martin's questions thundered through my head. *Is that the way I come across to people? Am I really like Paul?*

Slowly, I admitted the truth. Whenever Paul spoke in the group and I reacted, it was because I saw Cec Murphey in him. Yes, I conceded, Paul reflected me rather well.

I finally saw Paul differently. I examined those qualities in him that upset me. I didn't like what I saw, but I wasn't quite ready to surrender.

"Tell me honestly, Martin, am I overbearing and opinionated?"

"Sometimes," he said, "but I know you and like you."

After Martin left, I pondered what he had forced me to admit. For months, I had complained to God about that obnoxious writer. All the time, I was complaining to God about myself.

"I'm sorry, Lord." A wave of shame flowed over me. How could I be so blind about myself? Since then, I sincerely prayed every day for months, "God, help me accept the parts of Paul I see in myself."

That experience also helped me to know myself a little better, which enabled me to know God better. Or perhaps it was the other way around.

God, help me accept the unacceptable qualities in myself
that I see reflected in others.

Getting Our Attention

Like many others, I'm interested in a variety of things, but one or two take precedence. I'm a runner, and I've hit the sidewalks every morning for about 35 years. At one time I planned every day around my running schedule. My accumulated miles seemed more important than many of those significant things I needed to do.

I could say the same about reading. For as long as I've been able to pronounce the words in books, I've been captivated by them. Even now, I sometimes go on what I call a reading binge. A hunger for the printed word captures me and I will read two, three or even as many as six books within a week.

There are other issues, but those two examples say it well: Many things vie for my attention. It's true with all of us because that's human nature. I have friends who spend eight to ten hours a day watching TV. I know a teen who bowls and golfs on Wii for at least five hours every evening. On CNN, I saw pictures of a young couple in Japan who got so hooked on video games that their infant child died from neglect.

You and I are not as extreme as that couple, but most of us struggle with time-consuming issues. I rarely meet someone who doesn't comment or complain about not having enough time to do everything.

Even though we all have the same allotted time each day, we don't all use it wisely. And I'm not the person to teach a course on time management. I'm fairly self-disciplined but I wrestle with the same time issues as everybody else.

One day it occurred to me that I couldn't say, "I don't have time to . . ." What I really meant is that I didn't have time to do something that wasn't significant to me. In fact, I'll state it more strongly: We all have time to do everything we want to accomplish.

Some might want to argue with that, but I believe my statement. Because we can't always be honest with ourselves, we make excuses, we rationalize our behavior and explain to ourselves and to others the reasons we can't complete certain activities.

Too often we're being dishonest. We focus on the things we truly want to do and excuse ourselves from what we neglect. One friend said, "Some things demand attention, but I choose to ignore what some have called the 'tyranny of the urgent.' Instead of believing in 'planned neglect,' I choose the things not to do."

This has become an important issue to me because, for most of my adult years, I was a compulsive, task-driven individual. My wife used to shake her head and say, "You can't leave anything for tomorrow if you can possibly do it today." And she was correct.

I rushed a lot. The Africans called me *Haraka*, which means quick or speedy. I accomplished more than many others—and at one point that became a positive validation for me; however, in recent years, I've made a determined resolution to slow down and direct more energy into what's important to me as a person and as a child of God. Instead of focusing on how much I accomplish or how productive I've been, I think this way: Many things yell for my attention; fewer things grab my heart. I want to know the difference and decide to which I want to respond and include in my schedule.

I've made many fine choices since then and my life has become more balanced—not perfect and not yet everything I'd like it to be. But I'm learning to follow my heart. By that I mean, following the path that makes me a better person. Or I could say, the path that draws me closer to Jesus Christ.

I continue to return to one thought: When I do what's best for Cec, it not only makes me more knowledgeable about myself, but it also gives me increasing insight into the character of God.

As I become aware that God has become stronger or more important than other things, I know I've made the right choices.

Many things grab our attention;
fewer things grab our heart.
We need to know the difference
and decide which to follow.

Keep Me Humble

Shirley and I joined a small community church within a year of our marriage, and I enjoyed it. I knew everyone and liked the people. We attended two worship services on Sunday and Wednesday night Bible study—which was normal back then. At the midweek service, we studied the Bible for about 40 minutes and we had oral prayer time for the last 20 minutes.

Elderly Claude Puhl prayed every week, usually he was the first one, and I loved the directness and energy of his prayers. But one thing bothered me. Every time he led in prayer, Claude repeated one sentence: "Lord, keep us humble."

Over the next few years, I heard others use the same words, so I realize it wasn't an exclusive petition with him.

Those words bothered me because they didn't apply to me. I didn't consider myself a top-quality Christian (although that was my desire). Each time Claude prayed, I was reminded of my own pride and self-will. I yearned for the day when I could pray the same words.

Although Shirley and I haven't been involved in that church for many years, I can still hear Claude's raspy voice. Even so, I still can't pray those words.

About a decade ago, I wondered what secret Claude and others had learned that I hadn't. How did they know they were humble? What did they do to overcome their pride or their self-centeredness?

For years I avoided the word "humility." I sometimes laughingly said that I didn't consider it a virtue. What I really meant was that I never attained a state of humility.

And yes, I know the meaning of the word. It's not the trampled-upon person who takes everything from everyone and smiles. Sometimes people use the word "meek." It's not the person who gets in a long line at the post office and invites others to get in front of him.

James 4:7 exhorts, "Humble yourselves before God. Resist the devil, and he will flee from you." Some versions translate the word as "submit," which means to give ourselves unreservedly to God. I like that much better.

I yearn to know God and to obey him in every aspect of my life. Perhaps I'm too aware of my imperfections or feel I still have too far to go before I can call myself humble. Perhaps that's why I can't consider humility as something I've attained and want to clasp tightly.

Another thought comes to me: *Is humility something we don't know if we've attained?* Is it possible that the most humble are those who are quite unaware of that quality in their lives? Is it possible (and I hope it is) that the farther we see ourselves from claiming the label, the closer we may be?

This isn't any attack on Claude Puhl or anyone else. This is a self-scrutinizing view of Cec Murphey. He knows what he yearns to achieve, but he hasn't any idea how to know if he has attained that state. He likes to think that he's at least grasped a corner of humility and is slowly edging forward. So in the meantime, he prays, "God, make me totally submissive to you."

I don't pray, "Lord, keep me humble."
Instead I pray, "Lord, make me humble."

About Phil

"I suppose you know about Phil?" Ora said. "None of us have anything to do with him. It wasn't merely his divorce and quick remarriage, but all those stories about how he mismanaged money and the failure of his business and—"

"I prefer not to know," I said. I had become the pastor of the church less than a month earlier. My words might have been more tactful, but I stopped her gossiping further and she changed the subject.

That night in bed, I thought about what Ora had told me. Perhaps Phil was guilty of everything the church member implied. Perhaps he had committed a thousand other sins. Did he need pointing, accusing fingers? The question troubling me was not whether it was true, but *how* should I react?

I wondered how Phil felt. *Does he feel alone? Uncared for? Does he feel judged by others?*

Unable to sleep, I couldn't get beyond the shock of what I had learned. Lying there, I thought of the teachings of Jesus. In my mind I pictured the enactment of the Good Samaritan parable. Did the stranger, coming to the badly beaten Jew, inquire about his purity of life, his social conduct or his faith in God? Without asking questions, he bound up the man's wounds. The Samaritan realized the man needed compassion and healing.

The next morning, I called Phil. "I've heard a few stories and it's none of my business," I said. "I've called for one reason: I want to know you and care about you."

"Thanks for being concerned." His voice choked before he shared a few details of his situation, but only in the vaguest terms. Mostly he talked about his sense of alienation. "All those church members I thought were friends now avoid me in public. One of the men who used to be my closest friend told me he couldn't be of any help to me. He had also been a good friend to Nancy and said that to befriend me would be showing partiality and disfavor to her."

That seemed strange reasoning to me, but mostly I listened. In several different ways I tried to say, "I care." I also invited him to lunch at the end of the week.

After we hung up, I realized I had done what I could. As I prayed again for Phil, this thought came to me: *I eased his pain; God erases it.* And I focused on the story in John 8 about the adulterous woman brought before Jesus. The religious leaders expected him to enforce the rule of having her stoned. Jesus said one thing: "Let the one who has never sinned throw the first stone!" (John 8:7).

I sensed some of Phil's feeling of isolation and aloneness. Those whom he had expected to uplift him turned from him and pulled him down with their pointed fingers.

Had Phil's behavior been wrong? Was that the kind of conduct I could condone? Then it hit me: My responsibility wasn't to peep into his life, inspect his actions and question his motives. My responsibility was to treat him the way I would want to be treated if I were in a similar situation.

When I fail, I already have enough self-judgment and guilt without anyone else adding more. When I've come out of a situation in which I failed, I need others to encourage me, not make me feel worse. That's when I need hands stretching out saying, "I care about you."

Why can't we love people like Phil in the midst of their trauma? I wondered. Why does the enormity of others' failures horrify us?

They're only human too. Why do these things prevent us from caring? Why can't we extend the hands of compassion? Why do we wait until they've repented, straightened out or conformed to our standards of living? Now is when they need us.

Maybe some of them were afraid that what he had done was something they might be tempted to do and were repulsed to consider that.

Then another thought struck me. I had cared and extended a loving hand to Phil. *But how many times had I been on the other side? How many times had I stood with accusing fingers when people needed compassion?*

Lord, forgive me.

I'm not responsible to scrutinize others' motives and actions.
My responsibility is to treat others the way I'd like them to treat me.

Just Say No

"Just say no" is easy advice to give; it's not easy advice to follow. At least it hasn't been for me. Many times I haven't wanted to say yes, but I didn't know how to say no. Even when I declined, I often felt guilty or selfish, especially when the other person said, "You're so good at this" or "But it's only one hour a week."

For years, I admired individuals who could say no without apology. My wife is one of them. The first time I became aware of that ability was nearly 30 years ago. Shirley worked full time and struggled to finish her degree in journalism. A woman at church asked her to teach a Sunday School class. Shirley stared directly into the eyes of the asker and said, "No, I'm not taking on any more activities at this time."

The other woman started to explain how much the church needed Shirley's help. "I'm not taking on any more activities at this time," Shirley said. That ended it.

Our friend Betty Freeman, who had overheard Shirley, said to me, "I admire your wife for not feeling she has to give 50 reasons."

Betty realized that some of us refuse but feel we must justify our saying no. Many of us can't say simply, "No, thank you." (At least it hasn't been easy for me.)

Many of us seem compelled to explain, and perhaps because those words sound weak, we give a second reason and compound it with additional excuses.

We're caring people—faithful church members, and people-helpers—and others expect us to say yes to everything. (Or perhaps we mistakenly assume that's what they expect.)

When I turned down a request for a job I didn't want to do, I used to wonder if other people considered me lazy or selfish. As I've grown more comfortable with myself and less intimidated, I've learned to turn down requests without negative emotions tugging at me.

Eight years ago, I experienced my first significant victory in this area. I had taught several times in a writers' conference and liked the people who attended. One day, a board member phoned me. "We think you'd make a wonderful addition to our board of directors. Will you serve?"

"I appreciate being asked, but I don't think so." (That response in itself was a victorious step.)

"Our board meets only twice a year and we pay all expenses." She minimized the time away and maximized the benefits to me.

"Sorry, but my rubber band won't stretch any farther," I said.

"Oh," she said. "I understand."

That simple statement was a breakthrough for me. I didn't explain my reasons. (She would have tried to refute them anyway.) By giving a flat statement, I provided no argument for her.

And since then I've learned another lesson. If we say yes to things we don't want to do—even if they're good things—we take away our energy to devote to the things we need to do or want to accomplish.

I want to say no to things I don't like; I also want to say no to good things so that I can give myself to the excellent. It's not always that easy, but that was a beginning. I've since learned many lessons about saying no. I'm still learning.

If I say no to the bad or even the good,
I'm free to say yes to the excellent.

Secondhand Messages

Alton called me aside after Sunday School class. "You haven't seen much of Pete lately, have you?" he asked. Before I responded, he said "I thought you ought to know that you offended him by something you said about a month ago."

"Offended him?" I wondered what I could have said.

"One Sunday he tried to get into the church office but the door was locked. You came by and said, 'That's the first time I ever saw you trying to get *inside* the church.'"

I recalled the incident. Pete had joked about the pastor not being able to get to church early enough to unlock his office.

"I was only kidding him," I told Alton.

"That's the way Pete is." He told me several tales of Pete's touchiness.

"How did you find out he was offended?"

"He told his brother-in-law who told Bill, and Bill told me."

Typical story. Someone gets offended and by the time the information gets to the right person, it's been filtered through at least three other people.

The conversation bothered me. I had hurt someone, even though unintentionally. I reviewed the conversation in my mind, but I couldn't understand how anyone could have misconstrued the conversation. Yet Pete had.

"He ought to have come to me," I mumbled to myself. I heard the words echo back, "He *ought* to . . ."

Later that day, I grumbled to God. "I'm tired of innocent remarks getting twisted around and I get accused of hurting people's feelings. Why am I supposed to reconcile? People don't seem disturbed when they hurt *my* feelings. If Pete had been hurt, he was the one responsible to tell me."

I couldn't leave things like that. Likely, Pete had intended for the information to reach me that he was hurt. Although I felt I had done nothing wrong, the fact remained: Pete had been offended.

When I later apologized to Pete, he denied he had been hurt, but I knew better. However, that incident pushed me into serious thinking. Aside from the fact that Pete should have come to me himself, other things were also wrong. I heard the information through the I-thought-you-ought-to-know message system.

Haven't we actually twisted it from the principle Jesus gave? He said, "If another believer sins against you, go privately and point out the offense. If the other person listens and confesses it, you have won that person back" (Matt. 18:15).

Caring means being honest and confronting when necessary. It used to be that when conversations like those came to me, I kept the names in confidence. When I had to confront the third person, I'd say, "Someone told me that . . ." or "I've heard that . . ."

I determined to change the way I responded. Shortly after that, Fran cornered me after the worship service. "Go see Rita this week." Rita had been one of the most faithful members of my class.

"Any particular reason?"

"And ask about her father."

I nodded. I'm sure the puzzlement in my mind showed on my face.

"You hurt her feelings."

"What did I do wrong?"

"You didn't ask about her father. She was gone all last week. She told you he was ill and you had prayer for him in class. Now she's back and you didn't ask about him."

"I forgot. But why didn't she tell me herself?"

Fran shrugged.

"I'll contact her this week and ask about her father. I'm sorry I forgot. But you can help me if this kind of thing comes up again. Urge her to tell me herself."

"She'd be embarrassed and say it's such a small thing—"

"But it's not too small for her to get her feelings hurt. It's not too small for her to tell you so that you would be sure to pass it on to me."

"You're right," she said. "I'll try next time." I hope she did.

That's how the twist operates. One person does something wrong (even unintentionally). The offended one waits for the offender to smooth it out. If I'm hurt, I have an obligation to tell the person who offended me.

I've failed by allowing people to shirk their responsibility to each other. I made a promise to myself: No longer will I bear secondhand messages. I'll urge individuals to confront each other. I intend to care enough to help them be honest and faithful. I don't enjoy saying hard things to people. I'm as uncomfortable as the next person. If I care about the people involved, I can do it.

I don't like to get secondhand messages about my failures,
but I can't stop them.
I can stop giving out criticisms that will go to the
other person second hand.

"You Hurt Me"

"People around here say you're kind and loving." She stood up in the middle section of the auditorium. "Maybe that's how they see you, but that's not who you really are. You deeply wounded me and trampled on my feelings. I think you're cruel, harsh and thoughtless."

The crowd at my lecture had been especially large that night with more than 600 people in the auditorium. Her voice was loud enough that everyone heard.

"You're absolutely right; but that's not totally who I am," I said. "What others say about me is also true."

I assume she expected me to defend myself, because she looked confused. She stammered a few words but I couldn't hear them.

"If I were to characterize you right now," I interrupted, "I would say that you're judgmental, vindictive and mean-spirited. But I'm sure those who know you well would also say you have excellent qualities and they appreciate you."

Before she sat down, I said, "I'm sorry for your pain and also sorry that you've decided to become hurt over something I said or did."

"I decided? You hurt me! You trashed my writing and called my writing dull and immature. Why wouldn't I be hurt?"

"I'm sorry for your pain; I truly am, but my words stung because they hit one of your vulnerable places. If it hadn't been a sensitive, unhealed place in you, you would have tossed off my remarks."

Did that account really happen? No, it didn't. It's a revised scene from a work-in-progress novel. Sometimes I can say things in fiction that I can't when I write nonfiction.

I could have started this chapter by telling you about my own pain this past month. Four or five people sent me harsh emails, or as they say today, "They flamed me." Notice I call them harsh. The people who wrote those words would likely have called themselves honest, candid or forthright.

Even though I felt the sting of their words and became momentarily angry, in retrospect, I'm grateful for them. After a few hours of agony (because I'm sometimes a slow learner), I realized they had touched vulnerable spots in me. They penetrated places where I was susceptible. All of us have such places, and being fallible, imperfect creatures, we'll always have a few defenseless spots. That means when someone strikes there we feel hurt, we become angry, we want to defend ourselves.

If we can pull back a little, as I did (eventually), we see that their words enable us to accept areas we need to examine and to pray for God's help to overcome.

Perhaps we need to distinguish between their intentions and our responses, but I suggest not. Perhaps they intended to be mean or deliberately wanted to hurt me. That doesn't matter. What matters is my response.

This past month those people did me a favor by calling my attention to my defenseless vulnerable places. I wish I could learn such lessons a little more gently.

The words of others hurt when they strike my vulnerability.
They help me recognize the unhealed parts of myself.

Enough Appreciation?

"Everybody raved about my presentation," the speaker said to me. "At least a dozen people came to me to tell me that it was the best presentation of the conference."

I don't know how truthfully Rick spoke, but that statement was typical of him. He needed constant appreciation. If he didn't get it, he found ways to remind others of his immense talent.

A number of my friends avoided Rick whenever they could. They didn't want to listen to his self-praise, or they felt pushed to compliment him.

"Why does he have to tell us how talented he is?" one friend asked. "He wears me out. In every conversation, I feel I have to tell him how marvelous he is at least 10 times."

Another person said, "He's such a high-maintenance person. If he could only stop making every conversation focus on himself, I might learn to like him." He shook his head and said, "But how would I know? He doesn't give me the opportunity to make up my mind about who he is beneath all the bragging."

I agreed and realized that nobody ever gets enough affirmation and appreciation, and I admit he's high maintenance. He does annoy me at times, but I don't want to push him away. At least most of the time I can bear with him.

I know a little of his background: His parents never complimented him or praised any of his achievements. They complained, however, when he didn't perform excellently, because good was never enough. He had to be the best in everything he tried. I'm sure he feels worthless, although he'd never say that, and he must be aware of being ignored or rejected by others. He begs for a fix—for anything to make him feel better. It probably works temporarily, but it's not a long-term cure.

What's wrong with propping him up a little—as long as it's honest? To find words of encouragement and to speak them to that needy soul might begin to replace some of the emptiness from his childhood.

I can't solve Rick's problems, because he has needs that can only be satisfied from within and with God's help. But I don't have to push him away because he irritates me.

As I think of him, I'm reminded that I haven't always liked myself. Maybe that's why Rick presents a problem to me. His words have sometimes made me cringe, but they're often the kind of things I'd like to hear others say to me. I wouldn't be so gauche that I'd actually ask or say, "Tell me how wonderful I am." But I'd still like to hear such praise.

I've learned that the more I like who I am, the less I need affirmation. (Please notice I wrote *need* and not *want*.) It also took me a long time to value myself and I'm grateful to those who encouraged me when I didn't know how to accept myself.

Maybe we can help lift up such individuals with kind and encouraging words. We might also put the golden rule into action.

Nobody ever gets enough affirmation and appreciation.
It costs us nothing to honestly affirm others.

Self-made People

"He is a self-made millionaire," the host said as she introduced the speaker. For perhaps a full minute, she extolled his many achievements. She implied that he had started with nothing, had no human help and accomplished outstanding results in the business world. He became successful by only his own ability.

My response: *Impossible. No one is self-made.*

We all need help; we all receive help. We may not acknowledge it, but we've all had others who influenced and encouraged us. If we investigate the success of any human being, we realize that others assisted those individuals on their upward path. Some people intentionally reached out, others unintentionally encouraged them.

For example, I've thought about my writing career. I've earned a living as a writer since 1984, and not many writers live only on their income from writing. I guess that makes me successful. I've worked hard—and continue to do so—but that's only a fraction of the answer.

God sent many people into my life to make me who I am. The late Charlie Shedd said I had talent after he read a few articles I'd written. With his encouragement, I started an editing group called the Scribe Tribe. For nine years we helped each other learn the craft. With that group's critique, I sold more than 100 articles. Charlotte Hale was a member of the Scribe Tribe who told a book publisher about me. He read several of my articles and offered me a book contract.

I became a ghostwriter because Suzanne Stewart, another member of the Scribe Tribe, introduced me to Vic Oliver, then editorial director of a publishing house. I sent him a novel, which he didn't like, but he said, "You know how to get inside other people. I'd like you to become a ghostwriter for us." Under Vic's leadership, I wrote 35 books for that publisher.

In 1989, when most Christian writers didn't know there were literary agents, an agent called me. Vic Oliver had told him about me, and he needed a writer. After our discussion, I signed a contract, and he represented me for the next seven years.

Or I could take this from the point of view of my spiritual growth and point to many significant people who nudged, challenged or taught me. Earlier in the book I mentioned Barry Grahl's help in memorizing Bible verses. Shortly after I became a believer, John Burbank and I regularly walked four miles to church and debated theology along the way. Shirley Brackett (whom I later married) taught me the importance of setting aside time every day for prayer and Bible study. I've mentioned three people, and I could easily list a dozen.

So could most of us—if we pause to think about it. I am where I am today because of the individuals who touched my life.

This brings me back to the idea of being self-made or self-successful. No one makes it without the help of others. Some people don't like the idea of dependence on others or giving them credit, but that's the way God created us. We need them; they need us.

I'm reminded that the Protestant Reformers formulated what they called the "means of grace." Those "means" didn't guarantee grace, but they made it more accessible through such means (or methods) as reading the Bible or hearing it preached, prayer and the sacraments. The one I rarely hear mentioned today is "the communion of saints."

By that term, they meant that we grow in relationship with other believers. The simple act of being around other spiritually minded people influences us and teaches us. In the church, it means we call on each other when we need help.

I don't always feel like going to church, but I go. I need the people who hug me or shake my hand. Sometimes a simple smile brightens my day, or a congregational song lifts my spirit. Being in the presence of other Christians helps me to keep growing. I don't want to be self-successful. Instead, each day I pause and thank God for people who have contributed to my growth.

Here's the surprise to me: The more I've thought of those spiritual influencers, the more names come to mind. I used to think of four or five. Yesterday, I must have thanked God for at least 20 individuals.

Instead of being self-made, I prefer to thank God for the many people who have influenced me and helped me to be who I am now and continue to encourage my growth.

No one becomes successful without the help of others.
God, enable me to be one of those
who helps others become successful.

The Devil Did It?

Most of us have heard people say as a joke, "The devil made me do it." We've also heard individuals say, "The devil sure tormented me this week," and that's not a joke.

I have no problems with a personal devil or in evil forces at work in our world; I have problems with individuals who ascribe every failure to the devil. To blame the devil, or anything else, takes the easy way out of coping with our moral or ethical shortcomings. If we focus on outside forces as the cause, it enables us to look better and soothes our guilt.

Perhaps that's the problem: We don't want to face the pain of our failures or admit our sinful tendencies. If we select another villain, we don't have to look deeply within ourselves, confess or make any changes.

When things go wrong, it's natural for many of us in the church to point to the devil. We've been taught that he is *the* enemy. The book of Job starts when Satan (another name for the devil) challenges the Lord to step back and observe Job's character when the man has no divine protection.

Most people know that although that godly man lost everything, he held on to his integrity. At the end, God gave Job additional children and more possessions than he had before. With that understanding, some of us have learned to cry out when temptations strike, "The devil is tormenting me."

But what if we're mistaken? What if the problem begins in our thoughts? What if it starts with our sinful nature? What if we fail without any evil power taunting us? Instead of looking for culprits, what if we round up the nearest suspects—ourselves? What if we asked, "What's going on *inside me* to push me to do that?"

We're experts at pointing the blame away from ourselves because we had good teachers. Adam pointed to Eve and she pointed to the serpent, and the dodging of responsibility has gone on through the centuries.

We'll work hard to justify our innocence. That's human nature; however, I've learned that if I can focus on the issue long enough, I can usually ferret out the culprit—myself. Perhaps I was jealous. Maybe I held a deeply hidden grudge. Possibly someone belittled my skills.

Instead of looking at every threat or failure as satanic forces bumping up against us, doesn't it make sense to start within ourselves? If we want to bring in the devil, there's a place to do that: *After we've taken a step in the wrong direction.* That's when the evil influences spring into action. The devil works, but we have to provide the opportunity.

The apostle Paul urged the people at Corinth to forgive each other "in order that Satan might not outwit us. For we are not unaware of his schemes" (2 Cor. 2:11, *TNIV*). He warned that if they didn't look within and work out things among themselves, they were giving Satan an opportunity.

Here's an example that helped me understand how this works. More than 20 years ago I ghosted Velma Barfield's autobiography, *Woman on Death Row.* I documented at least 25 medical doctors who gave her prescription drugs during the time when she murdered four people. She never used the drugs (or the devil) as an excuse for her crime. "The drugs only brought out evil that was already inside my heart," she said to me.

That's how I like to think of failures, sins, wrongdoings—anything we do that's contrary to what we acknowledge as moral behavior. It begins with an inner weakness and a leaning toward doing something we know is unethical. Satan can take advantage of that, as the apostle said; but if we become attentive and pull back, the devil won't be able to make us do anything.

The next time I fail, I plan to say, "Cec made me do it." I think that would be more accurate.

We don't want to face the pain of our failures.
If we select another villain,
we don't have to look deeply within ourselves,
confess or make any changes.

Reasons to Dislike

I didn't like John for two reasons. First, he was unethical. He had taken advantage of two people I like. (I could have said *cheated* because it involved money.) Second, he was what my dad called a blowhard: a lot of loud noise with no substance behind it.

A few months ago, John and I were among two dozen teachers at a conference. Although I had no direct dealings with him, I was aware of his presence and realized how much I didn't like him. I began to pray daily for John. I reminded myself that it was the right thing to do.

Each morning I prayed for God to make him an honorable, ethical person. That continued for perhaps a month. One day I realized the obvious: What I disliked in John was what I disliked in myself. I want to be ethical but I realized that sometimes my motives aren't pure. I do right things for wrong reasons, such as say something kind when I don't feel particularly sympathetic.

The other part of John probably bothered me even more: his loud, empty words. It's not that I'd call my words empty, but sometimes I'm boastful or arrogant. I call attention to myself or more often to my accomplishments.

Again, I prayed for him, but I also prayed for acceptance of the John-part inside me. That went on for three or four months. And I want to be clear that John isn't the only person on my daily prayer list. I cried out to God for seven or eight people for different reasons, but all of them were spiritually deficient in some way.

One morning, I realized something radically new—at least new to me. I don't see myself as particularly insightful, and it takes awhile for me to grasp the obvious.

As I prayed for John and the others, here's the message I grasped. John and all the others are creatures of God. They're loved by God because—okay, because that's how God set it up. Again, obvious.

As long as I was critical of John, I was also critical of myself. It meant to me that there were still parts of myself that I hadn't accepted: parts of myself that I rejected or didn't like.

I still pray for John. But now, instead of complaining because of his lack of ethics, I ask God to help John overcome his problems. Instead of criticizing him for his failures, I can honestly say I want him to be blessed and happy.

I had one further insight on how to look at this. Jesus' words in the New Testament tell us to love others (neighbors) *as* we love ourselves. The word "as" means *on the same level,* and it also implies loving ourselves first.

For me, that means when I criticize others, I see it as a symptom of my own lack of self-acceptance. The qualities and actions I criticize in others help me to see my own self-love level.

The more self-loving I become, the more I can extend that love to other individuals. "Love your neighbor *as* yourself."

My attitude toward others is an excellent measure
of my own self-acceptance.

Setting Boundaries

More than 20 years ago, when I first heard the expression "setting boundaries," I didn't think much about the two words. But seven years ago I faced my need to do exactly that.

Without trying to blame parents or environment, I'll say I grew up without guidelines on where to erect fences to keep out prying and intrusive people. In our family, when anyone wanted a favor, we granted it. If someone asked a question—no matter how personal—we answered. I don't recall any of us saying, "That's none of your business."

Because I didn't know how to establish limits, people sometimes took advantage of me. For example, almost every week for years certain individuals phoned and took up immense amounts of my time. Or they asked me to do things for them I preferred not to do, but I did them anyway.

Seven years ago I promised myself, "I'll stop them from taking up all that time." It still took me awhile to figure out my strategy. For me, it was mostly being able to say no to things I didn't want to do. When someone asked, "Do you have a minute?" (and really meant, "Do you have an hour?"), I learned to say, "I have a few minutes." After perhaps 10 minutes, I can now say, "I have to hang up." Most of the time it works, although a few of those callers want to keep talking. After watching the clock for two more minutes, I say, "I really have to hang up now." And I cut them off. I don't like doing that, but they've overstepped my private property line.

I want to tell you *the* event that made me realize the need to set firm boundaries. I met Emma when I taught classes at a writers' conference. I skimmed a few paragraphs of what she had written and encouraged her to continue. A week later, she emailed me, "I've attached my manuscript. Critique it and tear it up as much as you need."

She didn't ask permission to send me her material. She didn't ask if I would edit it. She assumed I'd edit her work—all 293 pages.

I decided to wait at least a week before I answered. Three days later, Emma emailed to ask how I was coming along. "I'd like to send it to a publisher at the end of the month."

That actually happened (and it's not a once-in-a-lifetime event). I didn't know if I should rebuke her lack of manners, instruct her on professional conduct or ignore both her emails. Finally I wrote back, "I'm too busy." That was the wrong answer.

She knew I was busy, but "Surely someone helped you in your early days." After a few more sentences, she concluded, "If you'll work on the first three chapters that will be enough for now." (*For now?* I assume she still expected me to edit the entire book.)

I didn't reply and ignored two emails that followed. That was cowardly of me, but I didn't want more uninvited conversation. At first, I felt bad—really bad—about my response. But then, I thought, *I have erected a boundary.* I blocked her from trespassing. I hadn't done it well, but it was a beginning.

I'm getting better at it. I've learned not to explain, because some individuals respond by knocking down every argument. I wish I had learned that strategy 20 years ago. But the good news is that I can do it now.

It also occurs to me that if I take care of my own property and push away squatters, maybe I'll teach them to stay within their own boundaries.

Maybe they will.

If I set boundaries to keep out unwanted intruders,
that leaves more space for wanted friends and my best Friend.

Condemning Others

We know we're not supposed to judge others. That is, we're not to condemn others, think harshly of them or reproach them.

Most of the translations quote Jesus as saying, "Judge not," but one version reads, "Don't condemn others, and God won't condemn you. God will be as hard on you as you are on others! He will treat you exactly as you treat them" (Matt. 7:1-2, *CEV*). I don't like that translation because it makes it too personal. I can wiggle around and justify myself when I use the word "judge." But when I face "condemning others," I feel a divine finger pointing at me.

One of my friends read the paraphrase from *THE MESSAGE*: "Don't pick on people, jump on their failures, criticize their faults—unless, of course, you want the same treatment. The critical spirit has a way of boomeranging." Those words made it even worse.

Here's why I write about this. David Morgan and I meet almost every week for an hour or two. We attempt to be as transparent to each other as we can. I told David about a friend who had let me down and how much it hurt me. "He's thoughtless and indifferent," I said. "He didn't promise, but he knew what I wanted him to do." I used a few more unkind words about him.

David shook his head. "You were hurt because he didn't meet your expectations."

Naturally, I immediately rejected such an explanation. But as David continued, I dropped my defenses and said, "You're right." I had been emotionally wounded because I *expected* my friend to behave in a certain way—and it was something quite important to me. When he didn't follow the path I had envisioned, I felt justified in condemning him. I had set up the condition, and he failed.

Haven't most of us responded like that? We jump around to avoid admitting that we're judging. So we say it in a way that shows the weakness or failure of the other person:

- "He should have known I wanted him to . . ."
- "How could she not have realized that . . . ?"
- "He's insensitive about the feelings of others."
- "That's typical of the way she treats me."

If we can figure out how to thrust the wrongdoing on them, we're free, innocent and longsuffering. It may not be a sinful act to them, but it is to us, because we have judged it that way. (We wouldn't make that statement either.)

David forced me to think about my friend and others I've condemned.

How could they disappoint me unless I expected a specific action from them? If I expect a response, it means I've judged or decided how those individuals should behave.

To make it worse, too often, I *assume* others know. I've expected them to read my mind.

- "It's obvious how I feel."
- "She knows she deliberately hurt me."
- "If he wasn't so self-centered, he'd think more about others' feelings."

Don't the above statements sound a little crazy? Because I decide how they should act, and they don't follow my prescriptions, I am hurt and, consequently, I assign them a particular state of mind.

I can think of many instances when I have judged others. Harry came through town and didn't contact me. Joan and Tim had a party and didn't invite me. For years I gave Ron my newest book as soon as I received my author copies. He had his first book published and didn't give me one.

David's words have continued to force me to rethink my attitude. This morning this thought came to me. Jesus told a parable about rewarding those who did things for other people and that, in so doing, they were truly doing it for Jesus (see Matt. 25:34-40).

At first, I wondered if the principle applies in the negative: When I condemn others, I'm condemning Jesus. Or to put it another way, whenever I condemn or belittle anyone, I am giving Jesus Christ permission to use my measuring instrument against me.

I don't like that part.

I especially don't like it when I read the words of James: "Don't speak evil against each other, dear brothers and sisters. If you criticize and judge each other, you are criticizing and judging God's law. But your job is to obey the law, not judge whether it applies to you. God alone, who gave the law, is the Judge" (4:11-12).

As I read those words again this morning, I thought of the end of Jesus' parable about the religious leader and the tax collector, both of whom prayed.

The words of the cleric were: "I thank you, God, that I am not a sinner like everyone else. . . . I'm certainly not like that tax collector!" (Luke 18:11). Jesus contrasted that with the prayers of the lowly and much-despised publican: "But the tax collector stood at a distance and dared not even lift his eyes to heaven as he prayed. Instead, he beat his chest in sorrow, saying, 'O God, be merciful to me, for I am a sinner'" (v. 13).

The parable ends with these words: "I tell you, this sinner . . . returned home justified before God" (v. 14).

Yes, Lord, be merciful to me. I am a sinner. I don't like calling myself by that term, but it fits my conduct. Forgive me for my harshness and unkindness toward other people. Make me as kind to them as I want them to be to me.

Whenever I condemn others, I am condemning myself.
Whenever I judge others, I give God permission to judge me.

Forgiving the Unworthy

Milton was probably the most outstanding missionary I've ever known. He was zealous and visionary. For the six years we lived in Kenya, Milton was *the* authority. He had earned and deserved admiration for his achievements.

More than once I'd listened to him speak about his plans and felt overwhelmed. I'm an idea person in many ways, but he had the ability to see farther down the road of time and consequences than I did. I admired that about him.

Despite his many gifts, Milton didn't get along well with others. As one of them said to me, "No one works with him; everyone works for him." After I got to know Milton, I tried to avoid him whenever I could. He lived at the Kenya coast and I lived in the interior so we saw each other only a few times a year. But near the end of our time in Africa, we moved to the coast and worked together for a few months.

One time we had a disagreement and I was clearly wrong. I went to Milton, apologized and he forgave me.

We talked quite a bit and I said casually, "You're not really close to anyone, are you?" He admitted that was true. "Have you ever had a truly intimate friend?"

"Once," he said. "Once." He stared into the distance and added, "It was a long time ago."

When I asked what happened, Milton said only, "He betrayed me. I told him something in confidence and he told other people."

"Have you ever forgiven him?" I asked.

He shook his head. "He never admitted his wrongdoing and he never asked me to forgive him."

His words shocked me. "You mean, all these years and you've never forgiven him?"

"He knows what he did. If he wants my forgiveness, he'll ask for it. Then I'll know he's sorry and that he deserves forgiveness."

Since then, I've met several other people like Milton. They withhold forgiveness. Their attitude implies that it's within their power to forgive or not.

It's within our power to let those things go, but we lose if we don't forgive. If we hold on to a grudge or to someone's evil action, we're the wrongdoers. We feel the anger and the hurt and won't set ourselves free.

Sometimes we assume people have deliberately hurt our feelings (when they may not have) or that they're aware of the pain they've caused (and maybe they're not aware). As a result of those sad experiences, we hold the pain inside, and it grows. Or we compartmentalize portions of our emotions. One man had failed Milton, so he could never trust anyone else again.

Milton died a few years ago, and I wonder if he carried that one act of betrayal by his former friend to his grave. I don't know, but I sincerely hope he found a way to release his pain and set himself free.

Set himself free is exactly what I meant. I sense that when people say, "I'll never forgive ____," they consider it a threat of punishment against the offender. It's their way of saying, "You did something terrible but I'll have the final word in this."

I don't want to judge Milton or anyone else, but looking at this objectively, it makes me wonder about sin and forgiveness. Is it possible that Milton, holding on to his anger, his hurt and his sense of being betrayed, might have committed the greater transgression? Is it possible that if we weighed sins, the offender's betrayal would weigh less than Milton's grudge holding? Is it possible that Milton's attitude was far more grievous to God than that of the other man?

I don't know the answer, but from our conversation, I believe Milton had been hurt during his late teen years. He was in his forties when we met. That's a long time to carry a burden. That's a long time to hold on to pain.

I can only imagine the hurt Milton must have suffered whenever his betrayer's name rose in conversation or he thought of his once-close friend. No matter how wrong, how insensitive or how treacherous the friend had been, Milton was the real loser. He refused to release the inner torture.

And I wonder if Milton felt superior for holding on to his grievance. It was as if he were the noble one, ready to forgive— as soon as the other person asked.

"I'm sorry you feel that way." Those were the last words Milton and I ever spoke on the subject.

Over the years since then, when I've sung the hymn "What a Friend We Have in Jesus," I sometimes think of Milton when we sing these words: "O what peace we often forfeit, O what needless pain we bear."

Forgiving God, enable me to forgive those who have hurt me—
even if they never ask.

Difficult to Forgive

For most of my life, I didn't have a problem forgiving others. Except for one person. The one exception was someone from whom I expected—and demanded—the highest level of godliness and integrity.

The more I understood grace and realized how much God had done for me, the more kindly I felt toward others. Except for one person.

I learned to forgive those who wronged me even if they never apologized or tried to make matters right. Except for *him*. He didn't live up to the godly standards he professed. He hurt me countless times. No matter how many times I forgave him, it wouldn't be long before I had to scold, "You did it again."

He moaned and promised to change his ways. He meant it when he made that confession, but it wouldn't be long until he returned to his old ways. One time I was so exasperated, I confronted him. "Why do you keep sniveling like that? You did it again today and you'll do it again tomorrow and probably every day after that."

"I know, and I'm sorry," was all he said.

By now, it's probably obvious that the person I've had problems forgiving is Cecil Murphey.

What I wrote above is the way I felt. I can report, however, that I've been able to change my attitude during the past five years. Cec is still the same person, and he still says the wrong things, does dumb things and promises himself not to do them again. And he still fails, especially in the little things such as being kind or thoughtful. I've become more tolerant and compassionate. And definitely more forgiving.

That change began during a conversation with my friend David Morgan. I was concerned because I felt critical of several writers. I had trouble reading their books because I saw only their weaknesses and thought of ways I could have said things better.

"I'm not like that in the other parts of my life," I said.

David lovingly pointed out that the criticism I aimed at others was really the criticism I felt toward myself. I didn't like that answer, of course, and it took me at least two minutes before I could accept what he meant.

When I'm critical of myself, sometimes I express it by being judgmental of others. *Yes,* I thought, *I can see that in some of the people I know, and maybe I'm focusing on their weaknesses, but it's really my own that trouble me.*

I decided David was right.

Psychologists have long words to explain it, but I think of Jesus' words, " 'You must love the LORD your God with all your heart. . . .' A second is equally important: 'Love your neighbor as yourself' " (Matt. 22:37,39). The presumption is that self-love comes first. We can only give away what we already possess.

I can state that the more I accept myself (and forgive myself for failing) the more I'm able to understand, forgive and even encourage others.

Cec Murphey, I forgive you for being human and imperfect.

Forgiving myself is the hardest kind of forgiveness.

Being Alone

The Bible speaks of God's face, as in the blessing first given to Aaron: "The LORD make his face shine upon you" (Num. 6:25, *NIV*). Other biblical passages speak about God's watchful eye or his powerful arm or his ear that listens to us. We call those anthropomorphic terms—the biblical writers used those terms to try to explain God by using human characteristics.

But the one that means the most to me is the concept of the divine face. Not only does our Creator smile on us, but the Bible also speaks of God hiding his face, especially in the psalms. Does it mean God turns away? Or that we've been so terrible those holy eyes can't stand to look at us?

Perhaps, but why would God turn from *us*?

I have another explanation and one that has helped me. But first, I want to point out that I went through a period of 18 months when God hid his face from me. That is, I had no awareness of the divine presence, no sense of the Lord being with me. I searched my heart and cried out, but nothing worked.

I found comfort in biblical passages:

- "How long, LORD? Will you forget me forever? How long will you hide your face from me?" (Ps. 13:1, *TNIV*).
- "Do not hide your face from me . . ." (Ps. 27:9, *TNIV*).
- "Do not hide your face from your servant; answer me quickly, for I am in trouble" (Ps. 69:17, *TNIV*).

If we go back to the use of anthropomorphic terms, we realize that the poet cried out for blessings and assurances.

Because God remained silent or refused to answer, he expressed it by referring to God hiding his face—God looking away from us. That's the opposite of the benevolent smile.

Now that I'm past my time of God's hidden face, I've asked myself about the difference between God being with us and God turning away from us. Here are the questions I've asked myself: Is it possible that God may be closest to us when we're least aware? Can it be that although we have no perception of God, it doesn't mean God isn't present and guarding us?

In the famous story of Jacob's dream about the ladder and angels descending and ascending, he said, "Surely the LORD is in this place, and I wasn't even aware of it" (Gen. 28:16).

During my period of darkness, God was with me, even though I saw no outward evidence. I could see divine guidance only in retrospect. Afterward, I pondered my past predicament and I have been able to rejoice over the lessons I learned.

For instance, just because we sometimes feel alone doesn't make us alone. In fact, for Christians those dark times may be the moments of God's closest scrutiny in our lives. It may be a time for us to look deeply within ourselves and to examine our hearts. Those times may push us to overcome our complacency or to become aware of our dependency on God, or make us yearn for an even deeper commitment.

Said differently, but with the same idea of the turned-way countenance, we read of the Israelites in slavery in Egypt. "They cried out for help, and their cry rose to God. God heard their groaning, and he remembered his covenant promise to Abraham, Isaac, and Jacob" (Exod. 2:23-24).

Had God truly forgotten them? No one believes that, but their lives were arduous and the Egyptians were cruel. To their sensory evidence, God had become so busy in other parts of the universe that he had neglected or forgotten them. Not that they believed it, but it surely appeared that way.

In Psalm 44, the writer cries out for God to awaken. Was the sovereign Lord of the universe asleep? Hardly. "Awake, Lord! Why do you sleep? Rouse yourself! Do not reject us forever. Why do you hide your face and forget our misery and oppression? We are brought down to the dust; our bodies cling to the ground. Rise up and help us; redeem us because of your unfailing love" (Ps. 44:23-26, *TNIV*).

Because of my period of darkness, I've come to realize that whether I sense the divine presence or I don't, it doesn't say anything about the Lord. In fact, in the dark and dangerous times, God probably has to give us a little extra attention—but he does it by orchestrating events or doing the things that don't shout his presence.

I'll go further: When we've examined our hearts and believe we're as close to God as we know how to be—despite our human frailties—yet we have no sense of his presence, it may mean God is at our side, silently watching over us and always caring for us.

In moments when I feel most alone,
is it possible that God is the most present?

Victorious Living

I was the keynote speaker at a church, and afterward a number of people stood around in the foyer. They bought books and talked to me about my message. Their words affirmed me, and several individuals spoke about specific things I had said that ministered to them.

One man stood away from everyone else and I sensed he wanted to talk to me privately and would wait until everyone else was gone. That's exactly what happened. As soon as I began to pack away my books, he came over. "Could you spare a few minutes to talk to me?"

I agreed and we went over to an isolated corner. It took no prompting for him to open up. He told me about the loss of his wife to cancer, the death of his older son in Iraq and several other things. In a downsizing restructuring by his company, he lost his job. "I didn't work for nearly four months," he said.

After he told me his background and brought me up to the present, he said, "I want to be a victorious Christian, but I seem to fail regularly."

"What makes you think you're not victorious?"

"All those things I told you."

"But you survived, didn't you? You remained faithful to God."

"But where's the victory? I face problems all the time and—"

He said more than that, but I held up my hands. "The absence of problems isn't triumph."

He still didn't understand.

"I have no idea where you got your concept of triumphant living. Jesus assured his disciples that life wouldn't ever be problem free. 'I have told you this so that you may have peace in me. Here on earth you will have many trials and sorrows' [John 16:33]."

"Yeah, I know that," he said, "but the problems don't stop. They keep going on and on." Tears came to his eyes and he said, "And they're not problems of my own making. I feel sometimes that life is against me . . . that God's against me. I'm not giving up. It's just . . . just that I don't understand."

"I don't know why your life has become so difficult, and it sounds as if you've faced more problems within the past four years than some of us face in 40. But you *are* victorious. Many people want victory but they're not willing to fight for it."

He tried to interrupt me but this time I wouldn't let him. "Think what the word 'victorious' means. Can you conquer without having a battle? Can you win unless you have opposition? Victory means you overcome each obstacle. It doesn't mean a life without problems."

I opened his Bible and read, "Can anything separate us from the love of Christ? Can trouble, suffering, and hard times, or hunger and nakedness, or danger and death? . . . In everything we have won more than a victory because of Christ who loves us" (Rom. 8:35,37, *CEV*). Although I read the rest of the chapter, I saw the changed expression on his face when I finished verse 37.

He nodded several times and hugged me. I don't know how much he understood, but as he walked away from me, I thought he was probably one of the most victorious Christians I'd ever met. He had faced the major disasters in modern life and had kept on. Isn't that what Jesus means by giving us victory?

Victorious living doesn't mean a life free from problems;
victorious living means overcoming each problem.

My Improvement

I'm a product of my culture in many ways. Years ago, I became concerned about self-improvement. I never bought into the concept that I'm without limitation or subscribed to the human-potential movement that insists there is nothing we can't accomplish if we only put in the effort.

I did realize how important it is to push ourselves and work toward our highest potential. I also wanted to be a better me, and a more faithful disciple. I wanted every aspect of my life to show God's favor. Or I can say it this way: I wanted the grace of God to refine every aspect of my world. That's also biblical. "Grow in grace" is a theme in the New Testament. Peter put it this way: "Be on guard so that you will not be carried away by the errors of these wicked people and lose your secure footing. Rather, you must grow in the grace and knowledge of our Lord and Savior Jesus Christ" (2 Pet. 3:17-18).

Many New Testament exhortations are to move forward, to grow, to become better. That kind of growth doesn't mean an egotistical kind of self-improvement but to become the living example of God at work in us.

The problem is that too many people see self-growth as the purpose and the final end of the journey. For me, it's only the beginning. I became aware of that fact around 1988. I belonged to what we called the Men's Movement.

It was a loosely organized movement outside the church in which men learned to open up to each other. Many of them were lapsed church members who still believed in Jesus Christ but had lost faith in the church. For 10 years I remained with that men's organization. Structured as a loosely based mutual-help association, we were able to reach up and lift up others, and I also learned a great deal about myself in a safe, compassionate environment.

No one censured, jeered, scorned or made us feel weak or worthless. I found it refreshing to find such openness.

One thing struck me after I had been part of the movement for perhaps two years. Many wounded men came into our meetings. Over a period of weeks, sometimes months, they found acceptance and understanding. They faced their problems and became healthy. Some joined small groups, as I did, and many commented that they felt they had a new way to view life and wouldn't be the same again.

I believed them and congratulated them. Within weeks after their declaration of wholeness, most of them chose to leave. "I don't need the group" or "I've outgrown the organization" were common comments.

Their attitudes bothered me because I reasoned they were now able to help other broken, hurting men. Now was when they could lift up others and share what they had learned. But most of them seemed concerned only about themselves. (Not everyone left, but far more than stayed.) I remained active and continued to reach out to others. I had received loving acceptance and I wanted to pass it on to others.

That's when I realized an important principle: God wants us to improve (another word for "grow") but not only for ourselves. Once we've grown, matured, overcome—in the church, in business, in secular groups—we have the opportunity and the responsibility to help others and to remember how others helped us.

Lord, help me improve, continue to improve
and to use my improvement to help others improve.

Liking All of Me

I haven't always liked myself. I'll say it better: It hasn't been long since I began to love myself. It wasn't self-hatred, but more of dissatisfaction with myself and my spiritual progress.

I'm not at the end of my journey but I've accepted that I'm a spiritual work in progress. God started with raw, unwieldy material and at times I resisted.

In the early days, I had trouble accepting who I would become in the future. If I had failed so many times in the past and continued to fail in the future, what would my future look like? Yet, I assumed that I'd learn to live more consistently and that my life would honor God more.

My past troubled me, and I know that's common for many of us. We can't undo what's already happened or erase our mistakes. God forgives our mistakes, sins, wrongdoings, stupidity, rebellion or whatever we have chosen to call the unacceptable things behind us.

Even the past becomes just that: the things done and behind us. Over the years I've been able to look backward and accept my failures. Even though I'm ashamed of some of the things I did or said, I also realize that my loving Friend has taken those negatives and used them to positive effect. I understand God better and certainly know myself and, in the process, am more compassionate toward others.

It's the present that has given me the most trouble. And sometimes it still does. For example, after I had been a believer for 10 years, I still got angry and yelled. Occasionally I sulked because I didn't get what I wanted. After I realized my attitude, I confessed and asked forgiveness, but that didn't end the issue.

- "After all these years, I still do that?"
- "I should have known better."
- "I did it again, Lord, and I promised you I wouldn't."
- "I'm not as far along the Christian walk as I thought."
- "Lord Jesus, if I truly loved you, how could I have done that again?"
- "Won't I ever get control of my temper?"

The problem in the present became the problem of the past. That is, I reverted to former behavior and saw it as a continuum. "I did it again!" I yelled. I wondered how God could be so patient with me. (I still don't know the answer to that question.)

My spiritual state of mind didn't improve over the years. After I had been a believer 20 years, I cried out, "Lord, will I never learn? I should have overcome that by now." (I used "should," and realized I was laying more guilt on myself.) "If I live to be 97, will I still struggle with my temper?"

"Probably," I answered myself.

A few years ago, when I taught a Sunday School class called Bible Discovery, the question of forgiveness came up. I specifically remember answering Beth Wilson's question by asking, "When Jesus died on the cross, which of your sins did he take away?"

"All of them."

"Yes, the sins of the past," I said, "but what about the sins you'll commit next week . . . and you will sin again."

"Those too. They're all forgiven."

As she answered, I thought, *That's it. I'm already forgiven. I don't deliberately sin, but I will fail at some points—today or tomorrow or next year.* God continuously offers forgiveness, God never stops providing strength, but God doesn't demand sinless perfection.

I think of Psalm 103: "The LORD is compassionate and merciful, slow to get angry and filled with unfailing love" (v. 8). "For he knows how weak we are" (v. 14).

Because of that moment of insight, I started to pray each day: "Lord, help me love who I used to be, who I am now and who I am becoming." I've moved beyond asking. I'm now at the place of affirming that I've experienced the peace and joy from knowing that reality.

Jesus Christ has enabled me to lovingly accept every part of myself. I can embrace the Cec Murphey of the past because he did the best he knew how, even though he was often wrong. I accept him without reservation as he was, as he is and as he's becoming.

I like who I am, I like who I used to be
and I like who I am becoming.

My Favorite Prayer

One Sunday morning while I was still a pastor, I was ready to close the service with a benediction. Like most other churches, as soon as we finish the final hymn, the pastor blesses the people before they leave.

As we started the last stanza, my gaze shifted across the congregation. I have no words to express the feeling that came over me. I saw tired faces and eager looks. I yearned for them to be filled with joy and thanksgiving.

I had tried to preach an encouraging sermon and yet I wanted to say something more—anything—to lift their spirits and prepare them for the week ahead. As I stepped forward, I knew what to say.

"Before I pronounce the benediction this morning, I want you to repeat a simple prayer." They did exactly what I asked.

The first line didn't have much effect; but after I said the second, eyes popped open. Many people looked up at me and smiled.

Several members talked to me about that prayer. From time to time, a member of the congregation would ask, "Could we pray that prayer again?" And no matter how often I had them pray those 15 words, people responded. I think it's because it was a message they needed to hear. Or maybe it was a simple way for them to examine themselves and not see only their failures and shortcomings.

Although these words came to me more than two decades ago, they're still powerful, and I remind myself of them frequently.

Here is the prayer: "Lord, show me the truth about myself, no matter how wonderful it may be. Amen."

Most of us know our weaknesses. We probably have a few people around who gladly help us stay aware of our faults. *But what about our good qualities?* Too often we focus on what we're not—not spiritual enough, not loving enough or not sensitive enough. That's what many sermons and theological treatises told me, and I wouldn't argue with them. I would say only that I think they missed something important because they stopped too soon.

We need to accept our sinful nature, but we also need to move on and accept our noble qualities and the good things God has already accomplished in our lives.

To be more honest, too often when I preached, I felt members of the congregation missed what I yearned for them to grasp. They didn't need more thrusts with guilt harpoons or whips of culpability. They needed more embracing arms. Like me, most of them had been pursued by pronouncements of judgment and reminders that all of us come in at least a yard short of righteousness. I wanted them to accept their own divinely given goodness and to give thanks for the grace that was at work in them. They needed to accept their innate goodness.

Some people will hate that previous sentence and quote liberally from the Bible that "all have sinned" or "There is none good, no not one." And if we look at sinlessness or perfection, that's true. But if we're made in the image of God, as Genesis clearly tells us, isn't there something good left in us? The *imago dei* may be marred but not destroyed.

I posed a few questions to myself and to a few friends: What if we paused to give thanks to God for the good qualities in our lives? What if we thanked God because we care about people, we're musical, generous or we work hard? What if we began to thank God for making us who we are and to rejoice in his creation?

Each liked the idea. One 20-something man said, "Radical!" (which I understood as affirmation).

What if we gave thanks because "we are God's masterpiece" as Paul wrote in Ephesians 2:10? I've never heard a sermon on the topic of our being divine productions and great works of spiritual art.

That's when I continue to pray and to quote this simple prayer: *God, show me the truth about myself, no matter how wonderful it may be.*

That doesn't invalidate the need to know the good things about ourselves. I like who I am (and that journey took me many years), and I can now pray freely, "Thank you, God, for making me who I am. I'm not a finished product, but I sure like who I am already and I'm excited about who I'll become."

I want to know the truth about who I am; and if I'm a divine masterpiece, surely that makes me more than sinful, evil-thinking and low-minded.

Doesn't that remind us:

> *Loving God, show me the truth about myself,*
> *no matter how wonderful it may be.*

Aphorisms

1. I am passionately involved in the process; I am emotionally detached from the result.
2. God, heal the parts of me that don't want to be healed.
3. I'd rather be disliked for who I am than to be admired for who I'm not.
4. I am seldom angry about what I think I am angry about.
5. No matter how many times I examine the past, there's nothing I can do to make it different.
6. Today I have time to do everything I need to do today.
7. We can focus on those things taken from us or we can realize that loss can also bring freedom.
8. My role is not to solve others' problems; my role is to care about them while they solve their problems.
9. Grace builders are the difficult people who upset us and force us to pray more fervently and grow more quickly.
10. As I learn to accept myself, I learn to accept others.
11. I accept the unacceptable parts of myself.
12. When I yearn for what I don't have, I suffer; when I accept what God has given me, I am content.
13. If we love others, we will find ways to express our feelings.
14. God, help me remember others' acts of kindness to me; enable me to forget my acts of kindness to others.
15. My negative feelings are emotions; my negative feelings are not reality.
16. When I trust myself enough to be myself, others can respond by trusting me.
17. Our problems arise out of who we are. Although they come in different forms, the same problems find us no matter where we run.
18. Guilty people don't need a theology lesson on how to feel more guilty; guilty people need assurance of God's love and acceptance.
19. If I love you, and I think you're mistaken, it's all right; if I don't love you, and I think you're mistaken, I'll either reject you or try to fix you. It's easier to love you.
20. Lord, help me to realize I don't have to become lovable; you created me lovable.

21. It's impossible for God to love me more tomorrow than he loves me today.

22. "Forgive me," I prayed, "my will is so weak." God whispered, "No, your will is too strong."

23. When I try to show others that I am perfect, they see me as less perfect than I am.

24. It's easy to excuse our children for being thoughtless or careless. "They're only children," we say. I wonder if God sighs and says about us: "They're only children."

25. To me a problem may be minor, but to the person with the problem, it may be major.

26. God, forgive me for trying to make you into someone who helps me further my plans. Teach me instead to rely on you so that I can further your plans.

27. Have you ever noticed that God chooses unlikely candidates for service? I'm one of them. Maybe you are too.

28. If we know God is with us during the good times, why would we think God deserts us in the bad? Isn't that when God most shows he is with us?

29. God answers after we ask; sometimes God answers before we ask.

30. All of us want appreciation for our talent; we need appreciation for our personhood.

31. Obedience is required; understanding is optional.

32. I lovingly grant the Holy Spirit permission to use "ought," "should" and "must" in my life; to everyone else, they are forbidden words.

33. A true friend knows my faults, still loves me and has no plans for my self-improvement.

34. We can always teach others and share the knowledge and understanding we've learned. We can also learn from those we teach.

35. The best gifts come with no strings attached. In fact, only true gifts have no strings attached.

36. I give to others because it's good to do; I receive from others because it's right to do that. Both are acts of love.

37. I look like this because it's the face I've earned from the days I've lived on this earth. Each day my face declares who I am before I say a word.

38. No matter how many times I hear something, I will deny what I'm not prepared to accept.

39. Nothing of real value comes easily or quickly. Part of the value lies in the difficulty to reach it.

40. If I figure out a reason for God's love, I have the wrong answer.

41. Thank you, God, that you love me as much as you love other people.

42. God's responsibility is to guide; mine is to obey. Although I often remember my role, I sometimes forget God's.

43. God, remind me that today I can choose to redefine my life. Today I can start again.

44. When we compare ourselves with others, we feel we're losers; when we compare ourselves with Jesus, we know we're loved.

45. God, help me to do the right thing because it is the right thing, even when it's not convenient.

46. When we respond to God to guide through our superior mode, we don't make mistakes; when we listen to our inferior mode, we often fail.

47. Problems never leave us where we started. As we struggle with them, we can learn from them and grow.

48. If we focus on being who we are and refuse to let another's attitude upset us, we might actually change them.

49. God, help me accept the unacceptable qualities in myself that I see reflected in others.

50. Many things grab our attention; fewer things grab our heart. We need to know the difference and decide which to follow.

51. I don't pray, "Lord, keep me humble." Instead I pray, "Lord, make me humble."

52. I'm not responsible to scrutinize others' motives and actions. My responsibility is to treat others the way I'd like them to treat me.

53. If I say no to the bad or even the good, I'm free to say yes to the excellent.

54. I don't like to get secondhand messages about my failures, but I can't stop them. I can stop giving out criticisms that will go to the other person second hand.

55. The words of others hurt when they strike my vulnerability. They help me recognize the unhealed parts of myself.

56. Nobody ever gets enough affirmation and appreciation. It costs us nothing to honestly affirm others.

57. No one becomes successful without the help of others. God, enable me to be one of those who helps others become successful.

58. We don't want to face the pain of our failures. If we select another villain, we don't have to look deeply within ourselves, confess or make any changes.

59. My attitude toward others is an excellent measure of my own self-acceptance.

60. If I set boundaries to keep out unwanted intruders, that leaves more space for wanted friends and my best Friend

61. Whenever I condemn others, I am condemning myself. Whenever I judge others, I give God permission to judge me.

62. Forgiving God, enable me to forgive those who have hurt me—even if they never ask.

63. Forgiving myself is the hardest kind of forgiveness.

64. In moments when I feel most alone, is it possible that God is the most present?

65. Victorious living doesn't mean a life free from problems; victorious living means overcoming each problem.

66. Lord, help me improve, continue to improve and to use my improvement to help others improve.

67. I like who I am, I like who I used to be and I like who I am becoming.

68. Loving God, show me the truth about myself, no matter how wonderful it may be.

About the Author

Cecil (Cec) Murphey has written or co-written more than 120 books, including the *New York Times'* bestseller *90 Minutes in Heaven* (with Don Piper) and *Gifted Hands: The Ben Carson Story* (with Dr. Ben Carson). His books have sold millions and have brought hope and encouragement to readers around the world. Other books by Cecil Murphey include:

When a Man You Love Was Abused

Hope and Comfort for Every Season

Words of Comfort for Times of Loss

Christmas Miracles

When God Turned off the Lights

When Someone You Love Has Cancer

Everybody's Suspect in Georgia (fiction)

Heaven Is Real (with Don Piper)

I Choose to Stay and *Immortality of Influence*
(with Salome Thomas-EL)

Rebel with a Cause (with Franklin Graham)

Cecil Murphey enjoys speaking in churches and for events nationwide. For more information, or to contact him, please visit his website at **www.cecilmurphey.com**.